Our
Best Bites

MORMON MOMS
in the Kitchen

Our Best Bites

MORMON MOMS
in the Kitchen

Sara Wells & Kate Jones

SHADOW MOUNTAIN

To all Our Best Bites blog fans,

both those who have just joined us

and those who have been with us from the very early days:

This book would not have been possible without you,

and we love and thank you from the bottom of our hearts.

All food styling and food photography by Sara Wells
Art direction by Richard Erickson
Book and cover design by Sheryl Dickert Smith
Cover and author photos of Sara by Rebecca Smith
Cover photos of Kate by Lydia McDaniel Hutson
Author photo of Kate by Sam Jones

Text and photographs © 2011 Sara Wells and Kate Jones

Visit us at ShadowMountain.com

Library of Congress Cataloging-in-Publication Data
Wells, Sara (Sara Smith), author.
  Our best bites : Mormon moms in the kitchen / Sara Wells and Kate Jones.
    pages cm
  Includes index.
  ISBN 978-1-60641-931-1 (hardbound : alk. paper)
  1. Mormon cooking. 2. Cookbooks. I. Jones, Kate (Kate Randle), author. II. Title.
  TX715.W464 2011
  641.5'66—dc22
                                                                                          2010040573

Printed in the United States of America
Publishers Printing

10   9   8   7   6   5   4   3

Contents

Acknowledgments

Thank you to my sweet family, especially my boys, for suffering through many cold meals, and sights of goodies that couldn't be eaten, because everything had to wait to be photographed! Thank you to my wonderfully supportive husband, Eric. Eric, I appreciate so much the endless amount of energy and excitement you share about my hobbies and interests. I couldn't have completed this project without your support, encouragement, and patience. Thank you to my parents, especially my mother, who taught by example the value of gathering the family around the dinner table. Mom, thank you for the many years of love and the millions of dirty dishes washed. They are noticed and appreciated! A big thanks to my little sister, Becca, who is often the silent assistant in my projects. Thank you, Becca, for helping me brainstorm, for editing my grammar, and for sharing your amazing creative talents. Lastly, thank you to my partner in crime—Kate! How grateful I am for our surprise friendship and where it has taken us thus far.

Sara Wells

A huge thank you to Sara, for being an amazing blog and business partner, not to mention a wonderful friend! I also want to thank my wonderful family and friends, wherever you may be, for your love, encouragement, and support—I truly love you all. Thank you, Young Women of the Alexandria and Pineville, Louisiana, Wards—you guys were my ultimate taste-testers, kid-watchers, and hug-givers. Thank you to my parents, particularly my dad, for letting me scramble the eggs every morning and for reading me a book every night. Thank you, Dad, for being unfailingly supportive of me and whatever my dreams may have been at any given time, because that support of those dreams has led me here. Clark and Meredith, thank you for your sweet patience and love during the time I've spent working on this book. Finally, I want to thank my husband, Sam, who has been my greatest supporter, who picks up the slack and has never complained (at least not very loudly) when we have cereal for dinner because I've been too busy writing about food.

Kate Jones

Hello! We are Sara Wells and Kate Jones and we want to welcome you to our little cookbook! We are good friends whose paths crossed many times long before we ever knew each other. When Kate's husband, Sam, and Sara grew up in the same ward (and when Sara became best friends with Sam's little brother, Seth), no one had any idea that, years later, we, as new moms, would bump into each other on an Internet message board. We became fast (yet anonymous) friends because of our similar senses of humor, tastes in TV, and cooking styles.

In the spring of 2008, we started a little recipe blog. It was never intended to be more than a way of sharing our favorite recipes with our families and friends; after all, with one of us in Idaho and the other in Louisiana, and because we both had very little kids, we didn't really believe that it could be anything more than that.

Over those first few months, our friends and families told their friends and families, and our blog began to grow. We changed our name from "The Daily Bite" to "Our Best Bites" and found that even as our readership grew, really, at the heart of it, we are just two moms trying to make it work every day, which is something that keeps both us and our blog very real.

We both come from different cooking backgrounds, but we both arrived at essentially the same place:

cooking fresh, fun, flavorful meals that won't destroy our grocery budgets and don't require a lot of work.

In this cookbook, we've included favorite recipes from our blog as well as over forty new recipes. Additionally, we've included tips, both big and little, that will make your life easier in the kitchen. Because we both spent a lot of time as broke college students, we hate wasting ingredients, so we've included an index of rollover ingredients. That way, if you buy a bunch of cilantro or a quart of buttermilk that you need to use up, check out the index for other recipes that use those and other perishable (and slightly unusual) ingredients.

Generally speaking, our recipes are based on the best basic ingredients—when we say "butter," we mean real butter, like from a cow; and lime and lemon juice we like freshly squeezed, not from a bottle. We love the taste of kosher salt and freshly ground black pepper. We really feel like it's these simple changes that make people fall in love with (or rediscover their love for) cooking and eating at home.

We are so thankful to those who have supported us during the past few years. Please enjoy our cookbook and, if you haven't already, come join us and our friends at www.ourbestbites.com!

Love, from our kitchens to yours,

Sara Wells and Kate Jones

Appetizers and Drinks

Drinks

Facing page: Caramel Apple Cider, see page 27

●●●●●●●●●●●●●●●●

TIP: If the texture of cottage cheese bothers you, you can blend it in a food processor with the mayonnaise before mixing with the other ingredients.

SERVING SUGGESTION:
Serve with crisp vegetables.

Dill Dip

This is a good, basic veggie dip that's a great alternative to ranch. Cottage cheese adds both texture and protein.

½ cup mayonnaise	1 tablespoon dried minced onion
1 cup small-curd cottage cheese	2 teaspoons parsley flakes
1 tablespoon dried dill	⅛ teaspoon seasoned salt

Combine all ingredients. Chill for at least 2 hours before serving.

Hot Spinach and Artichoke Dip

If you're not crazy about spinach, feel free to leave it out. Either way, this cheesy, flavorful dip is perfect for big parties or small family fun nights.

Serves 12–16

☆ **Make Ahead**
🌿 **Vegetarian**

1 (9-ounce) box frozen spinach, thawed and drained

1 (8-ounce) package cream cheese, softened

1 cup mayonnaise

1 cup sour cream

2 cloves garlic, pressed or finely minced

1 tablespoon fresh lemon juice

1 teaspoon hot sauce

2 teaspoons dry parsley

¼ teaspoon black pepper

¼ teaspoon kosher salt

1 (15-ounce) jar marinated artichoke hearts, drained and chopped

1 cup grated Parmesan cheese

●●●●●●●●●●●●●●●●

TIP: This can be assembled 1–2 days ahead of time, covered tightly, refrigerated, and then baked for an additional 5–10 minutes.

SERVING SUGGESTIONS:
Serve with crackers, vegetables, baguette slices, tortilla chips, or pita chips (p. 7).

1. Preheat oven to 350 degrees F.

2. Use a clean dry cloth to squeeze all moisture out of spinach and then roughly chop. Place in a medium bowl. Add the cream cheese, mayonnaise, and sour cream and mix well. Add remaining ingredients and stir to combine.

3. Place in an 8 x 8-inch or 9 x 9-inch pan and bake for 35–45 minutes or until hot and bubbly.

Makes about 1½ cups

☆ **Make Ahead**
☉ **Quick and Easy**
🌾 **Vegetarian**

●●●●●●●●●●●●●●●●

TIP: Tahini can be a little expensive, but it also goes a long way. If you have a hummus-loving friend, you can always split it with them. Look for it in the Mediterranean and/or kosher food sections of the grocery store.

SERVING SUGGESTIONS:
Serve with pita chips, crackers, flatbread, or vegetables.

Hummus

Garlicky and savory, this healthy, addictive dip is delicious with warm, homemade flatbread or pita bread, crisp vegetables, or pita chips. Try spreading it on a bagel and top it with lettuce, tomatoes, red onions, and sprouts.

1 (15.5-ounce) can chickpeas (garbanzo beans), drained and rinsed

1 large clove garlic, minced

3 tablespoons fresh lemon juice

3 tablespoons tahini

½ teaspoon kosher salt

⅛ teaspoon black pepper

½ teaspoon cumin

⅛ teaspoon ground red pepper

4–6 tablespoons water, divided

3 tablespoons extra-virgin olive oil

1 tablespoon minced fresh parsley, optional

1. Combine chickpeas, garlic, lemon juice, tahini, salt, pepper, cumin, red pepper, and 3 tablespoons of the water in a food processor. Process until smooth. With processor running, pour in olive oil. Process until just combined. Add additional water by tablespoon until you reach the consistency you like.

2. Place in an airtight container and store in the refrigerator. For optimal flavor, refrigerate for at least 2 hours before serving. Right before serving, top with a drizzle of extra-virgin olive oil and chopped fresh parsley.

How to Make Pita Chips

Pita chips are an easy and healthy pairing with all kinds of dips like Hot Spinach and Artichoke Dip (p. 5) or Hummus (p. 6). Feel free to customize these chips to your own tastes!

Makes 32 chips

4 whole pita breads, either white or whole wheat
1 tablespoon olive oil
1 teaspoon kosher salt

1. Preheat oven to 350 degrees F. Line a baking sheet with aluminum foil and set aside.
2. Use a pizza wheel to cut each pita into 8 triangles. Drizzle olive oil over the cut pitas and toss with your hands to coat each piece.
3. Place the wedges in a single layer on the lined baking sheet and sprinkle with salt.
4. Bake for 15–20 minutes or until the chips are lightly browned and crisp. Cool completely before serving. Store in an airtight container.

VARIATIONS: Sprinkle your favorite herbs and spices on the pita wedges when you sprinkle them with salt. For a Greek-inspired chip, try using garlic powder, oregano, and basil. A sprinkling of cumin is a great match for hummus. For Mexican-inspired chips, try onion and chili powders.

Makes 1½ cups

⊙ **Quick and Easy**

●●●●●●●●●●●●●●●●

VARIATION: Add 1 teaspoon cinnamon and a generous pinch of nutmeg. In addition to the fruit, you can serve this in a hollowed-out pumpkin with Cinnamon Chips (p. 14).

SERVING SUGGESTION: Serve with assorted fruit; this is especially delicious with tart apple slices.

Caramel Toffee Fruit Dip

This is a great quick snack to throw together in a pinch. Tart Granny Smith apples are perfect for dipping into this creamy, caramely dip.

1 (8-ounce) package cream cheese, softened (you can use light cream cheese)

¾ cup brown sugar

1 teaspoon vanilla (you can add more to taste)

Toffee bits (found in the baking goods section of your grocery store. Try and find the chocolate-covered ones if you can! Your dip won't be pretty, but it will sure taste good!)

Combine cream cheese, brown sugar, and vanilla. Add desired amount of toffee bits.

Fluffy Orange Fruit Dip

This fruit dip is a great, fresh-flavored alternative to the Caramel Toffee Fruit Dip on p. 8. Try serving this with skewers of fresh fruit.

Makes about 2 cups

⊙ **Quick and Easy**

1 (8-ounce) package cream cheese

2 teaspoons orange zest

3 tablespoons fresh orange juice (just use some juice from the orange that you zested)

¼ teaspoon vanilla

Pinch of salt

1 (7-ounce) jar marshmallow cream

●●●●●●●●●●●●●●●●●

SERVING SUGGESTION:
Serve with any fresh chopped fruit; it's particularly delicious with strawberries, bananas, and pineapple.

Beat cream cheese, orange zest, orange juice, vanilla, and salt until smooth and creamy. Add marshmallow cream and beat until combined.

How to Roast a Red Pepper

If you have lots of red peppers from your garden, this is a great way to use them up!

Red peppers

Foil-lined cookie sheet

1 large zip-top bag, a bowl with plastic wrap, or a brown paper lunch sack

1. Preheat broiler to high.

2. Cut the tops off of the peppers. You want the segments to lie flat on the cookie sheet, so cut off the rounded tops and use them in another recipe (or as a snack!).

3. Remove the seeds and membranes and then slice the pepper into segments length-wise and lay skin side up on a foil-lined cookie sheet.

4. Place the oven rack on the highest position in oven and place peppers directly under the broiler. (You may want to open a window or a door in case you have a sensitive fire alarm!) Keep the oven door cracked and keep an eye on the peppers. You want them to be charred and blackened. It's okay if there are still some red spots, but you want even charring over all of the pieces. Move the pan around if you need to. See photo for how they should when done.

5. Take the peppers out of the oven and use a pair of tongs to immediately place in a zip-top bag and seal it. You can also place them in a bowl with plastic wrap securely on top, or in a brown paper bag folded over to keep the steam in. Set them aside and don't open them for any reason!

6. After about 20 minutes, the peppers should be cooled off enough to handle. Remove the charred skins from the peppers. They should slide right off without a problem. Toss the skins and you're left with beautiful, smoky-sweet roasted peppers.

ALTERNATE METHOD: Whole peppers can be roasted on the grill or directly on the flame of a gas range rather than broiled in the oven; just be sure to turn them frequently. When blackened, follow steps 5–6.

VARIATION: Try combining peppers with olive oil, garlic, balsamic vinegar, and fresh herbs and store in the refrigerator.

SERVING SUGGESTIONS: Slice and serve on sandwiches, or add to omelets, salads, dips, or anything that calls for roasted red peppers or even sun-dried tomatoes.

Roasted Red Pepper Dip

Serves 6–8

We have actually seen people fight over who gets the last of this dip! It's especially delicious spread on warm slices of sourdough baguette, but it's also great on chunks of bagel, French bread, or tortilla chips.

ROLLOVER
Roasted red peppers

1 (7-ounce) jar roasted red peppers
(about 1 cup diced)

¾ cup mayonnaise (low-fat works great)

1 (8-ounce) package cream cheese,
softened (low-fat works great)

2 tablespoons minced onion

3 cloves garlic, minced

1 tablespoon Dijon mustard

12 ounces shredded pepper jack cheese

TIP: If you have leftovers, reheating them in the microwave may affect the texture, so if possible, reheat the dip in the oven.

SERVING SUGGESTIONS:
Serve with soft, warm baguette slices, slices of sourdough bread, tortilla chips, pita chips, crackers, bagel pieces, or veggies.

1. Preheat oven to 350 degrees F.

2. If using bottled peppers, remove them from the jar and blot the excess water with paper towels—a lot of excess moisture will affect the texture of the dip. Dice the peppers and set aside.

3. Combine the mayonnaise, cream cheese, onion, garlic, and Dijon mustard. Add in the shredded cheese and the diced peppers. Place in an 8 x 8-inch (or similar size) dish like a pie plate. At this point, you can cover it and refrigerate the uncooked dip for up to 2–3 days.

4. Place in the oven and cook for 30–45 minutes. Baking time depends on the size of the dish used. Remove from the oven when the dip is golden and bubbly on top. Serve immediately.

Makes about 2½ cups

☺ **Quick and Easy**
🌿 **Vegetarian**

ROLLOVERS
Green onions
Fresh cilantro

Quick and Easy Salsa

If you don't want to make a giant batch of salsa but don't want to open a store-bought jar, or if you're not up for cooking, this blends together in a matter of minutes. It will keep for about 4–5 days.

2 fresh tomatoes, diced

1 (14.5-ounce) can diced tomatoes

1 clove garlic, minced

⅓ cup sliced green onions

3 tablespoons chopped cilantro

¼ teaspoon chili powder

1 medium lime, juiced

Kosher salt

Freshly ground black pepper

Combine fresh tomatoes, diced tomatoes, garlic, green onions, cilantro, chili powder, and lime juice. Season with salt and pepper to taste. Leave as is or pulse in a food processor or blender until desired consistency is reached.

Black Bean and Mango Salsa

This salsa is a unique blend of sweet and salty. It can be used as a dip, as a side salad, or spooned over meat. Try it with Grilled Taco Chicken (p. 114) or Chili-Lime Steak (p. 124) folded in Flour Tortillas (p. 37).

1 (15.5-ounce) can black beans, rinsed and drained

1 medium mango, peeled and diced (about 1 cup)

½ cup diced red onion (about ½ medium onion)

½ cup chopped fresh cilantro

2 tablespoons fresh lime juice

2 teaspoons red wine vinegar

½ teaspoon sugar

¼ teaspoon garlic powder

¼ teaspoon kosher salt

⅛ teaspoon black pepper

1 medium avocado, diced

1. In a large bowl, combine the black beans, mango, red onion, and cilantro.

2. In a small bowl, combine lime juice, vinegar, sugar, garlic powder, salt, and pepper. Stir to dissolve the sugar and then pour over black bean mixture. Cover and chill in the refrigerator for at least an hour.

3. When ready to serve, gently fold in the diced avocado. Season with additional salt and pepper to taste.

Makes about 2½ cups

☆ **Make Ahead**
☉ **Quick and Easy**
🌿 **Vegetarian**

ROLLOVERS
Red onion
Fresh cilantro

●●●●●●●●●●●●●●

SERVING SUGGESTIONS:
Serve with tortilla chips, or spoon over grilled chicken, steak, or fish.

🌿 **Vegetarian**

ROLLOVER
Flour tortillas

Sweet Fruit Salsa with Cinnamon Chips

A rainbow of fruits are tossed together and served with crispy, cinnamon-sugar-dusted flour tortilla chips.

Fruit Salsa

1 tablespoon honey

1 teaspoon fresh lemon or lime juice

⅛ teaspoon cinnamon, optional

4 cups diced fruit (whatever is in season; for prettiest presentation, use a variety of colors)

1. Whisk together the honey and lime or lemon juice. Mix in the cinnamon, if desired.

2. Carefully combine the diced fruits. Toss gently with the honey mixture and serve immediately.

Cinnamon Chips

1 tablespoon sugar

⅛ teaspoon cinnamon

6 (6-inch) tortillas

1½ tablespoons butter, melted

1. Preheat oven to 350 degrees F.

2. Combine sugar and cinnamon and set aside.

3. Lightly brush one side of each tortilla with melted butter.

4. Sprinkle with the cinnamon sugar.

5. Use a pizza cutter to cut tortillas into wedges.

6. Place the wedges on an ungreased baking sheet and bake for about 10–12 minutes, or until they turn a light golden color and the edges curl up.

7. Remove from oven and let cool. Serve immediately, alone or with Fruit Salsa.

Fresh Fruit Bruschetta with Orange-Honey Cream

Light and fresh, try making this for breakfast or brunch. You can substitute any of your favorite fruits in place of the fruits listed.

1 baguette or similarly sized French bread loaf

4 tablespoons butter, melted

2 tablespoons sugar

½ teaspoon ground cinnamon

½ cup sour cream

3 tablespoons honey

1 teaspoon orange zest

1½ cups diced strawberries (about 10 medium strawberries)

1 cup finely diced mango (about 1 medium mango)

1 cup finely diced kiwi (about 3 kiwis)

1. Preheat oven to 400 degrees F. Slice bread into ½-inch slices. Place in a single layer on a foil-lined baking sheet. Use a pastry brush to brush each piece with melted butter. Combine sugar and cinnamon and sprinkle evenly over bread slices. Bake for 10–12 minutes or until edges are toasted. Set aside to cool.

2. While bread is toasting, combine sour cream, honey, and orange zest. Stir to combine and place in the fridge.

3. Gently combine strawberries, mango, and kiwi. When the bread is cooled, place about 1 tablespoon of fruit mixture on top of each toasted bread slice and drizzle with sweetened sour cream mixture. If needed, thin the sour cream sauce with ½–1 teaspoon orange juice. Garnish with mint leaves if desired. Serve immediately.

Makes about 16 slices

ROLLOVER
Sour cream

●●●●●●●●●●●●●●●●

SERVING SUGGESTION:
Serve with Breakfast Taquitos with Lime-Chipotle Dip (p. 56) and Strawberry Cheesecake Bars (p. 216) for a perfect brunch!

How to Choose & Cut a Watermelon

If your watermelons have been nothing but lemons, check out this tutorial on how to pick a winner and then a super-easy way to cut it!

CHOOSING A WATERMELON

1. Make sure you're buying the watermelon in season. In other words, buy it in the summer, from about May through September. Watermelon is usually at its best when it's least expensive.

2. It should be heavy for its size.

When you start picking up watermelons, look for one that, when you pick it up, you think, "Something this size should not weigh this much!"

3. It should sound hollow.

Once you find your unusually heavy melon, put it down and knock on it. If it sounds hollow, you probably have a winner. A hollow melon alone doesn't mean it will be good, but one that's hollow and heavy is another story.

4. Examine the rind. Make sure it's not leaking, bruised, or soft anywhere. Also, look for a light yellow or white spot on the rind (which means it's ripe) and light brown "scabs" (which indicate sweetness).

CUTTING A WATERMELON

A lot of people don't buy watermelon, even if they love it, because they can't quite figure out a good way to cut it and eat it. We think slices of watermelon are fun, but for overall simplicity, we like cutting it into chunks. And this is the easiest way to do it.

1. Wash the watermelon. It sounds weird, but watermelons grow on the ground and the rind is dirty. When you cut into it, all the germs on the outside of the watermelon will make their way to the inside of your perfect watermelon.

2. Cut the watermelon in half and then into quarters.

3. Make vertical cuts about 1½ inches apart all the way down to the rind.

4. On one side, make horizontal cuts about 1½ inches apart.

5. When you do it correctly, you get perfect little cubes.

6. Flip the wedge over and let all the cubes that have been completely cut fall into a large bowl. There will be some pieces remaining.

7. Run your knife along the inside of the rind to release any remaining cubes. Repeat steps for remaining wedges.

Cream Cheese-Filled Strawberries

Sweetened, flavored cream cheese is piped into fresh strawberries in this elegant treat.

2 pints strawberries (with long stems, if you can find them)

1 (8-ounce) package cream cheese

¾ cup powdered sugar

1 teaspoon almond extract

¼ cup semisweet or dark chocolate chips, optional

½ teaspoon shortening, optional

1. Rinse and dry the best-looking strawberries you have. (You can let them air-dry on a clean kitchen towel if you're not pressed for time.) Set aside.

2. To prepare the filling, beat the cream cheese, powdered sugar, and almond extract with an electric mixer on high. This step can be done 2–3 days ahead of time; just place the cream cheese mixture into an airtight container and refrigerate. When ready to serve, spoon the mixture into a decorating bag fitted with a star tip.

3. Using a sharp knife, cut a strawberry from tip almost to the stem in the middle of the strawberry. Make another cut crosswise, making an "X." Be careful not to cut all the way through the strawberry. If the strawberry is sitting on its stem, it should flare open. Repeat this step with the remaining strawberries.

4. Using the filled decorating bag, gently pipe the cream cheese filling into each strawberry. Serve immediately.

5. If desired, place the chocolate chips and shortening in a small zip-top bag and microwave for 20–30 seconds or until the chocolate is melted. Making sure the top is sealed, mash the bag together to combine the melted chocolate with the melted shortening. Cut a small corner off the bag and drizzle the chocolate over the filled strawberries. Immediately place strawberries in the freezer or refrigerator to harden the chocolate quickly and then serve immediately.

Makes about 40 sausages

🍲 **Slow Cooker**

●●●●●●●●●●●●●●●

TIP: These are great straight off the pan, but they're even better if you place them in a slow cooker set to low. Not only does this make them taste amazing, but it's a great way to serve them at a party.

Bacon-Wrapped Mini Sausages

You won't be able to make enough of these to keep party guests happy!

1 (14-ounce) package Lit'l Smokies
1 (12-ounce) package lean bacon
¾ cup brown sugar

1. Preheat oven to 325 degrees F. and line a baking sheet with aluminum foil. Using a pair of kitchen shears, cut the slab of bacon into thirds.

2. Wrap one-third of a slice of bacon around a sausage, secure with a toothpick, and place on the baking sheet.

3. Repeat with remaining sausages and bacon. Sprinkle brown sugar over sausages and bake for 40–45 minutes or until bacon has cooked and is starting to brown. Serve.

Sweet and Sour Appetizer Meatballs

Tangy chili sauce and sweet grape jelly doesn't sound like a match made in heaven, but you'll be surprised that these quick and easy meatballs or mini sausages will be gone before you know it!

1 (12-ounce) jar chili sauce
1 (16-ounce) jar grape jelly

2 pounds frozen meatballs

Combine jelly and chili sauce in a slow cooker and stir until smooth. Heat the mixture if needed to combine. Add meatballs and set temperature to low. Cook for 2–5 hours on low. Serve with toothpicks.

Makes 16–20 appetizer servings

⊙ **Quick and Easy**

●●●●●●●●●●●●●●●●

VARIATION: This sauce is also great with 2 to 3 packages of mini sausages.

🌿 **Vegetarian**

ROLLOVERS
Parmesan cheese
Mushrooms
Green onions

Spinach and Parmesan Mushroom Caps

White mushroom caps are stuffed with a cheesy, garlicky mixture of savory ingredients and baked until tender in this Italian-inspired appetizer.

18 large fresh mushrooms, cleaned

2 tablespoons butter

4 cloves garlic, minced

¼ cup finely chopped green onions

1 (10-ounce) package spinach

2 tablespoons chopped fresh parsley

1 (6-ounce) jar marinated artichoke hearts, drained and chopped

6 ounces (about 1½ cups) freshly grated Parmesan cheese

¼ teaspoon kosher salt

Black pepper to taste

1. Preheat oven to 350 degrees F. Line a baking sheet with aluminum foil and spray with nonstick cooking spray. Set aside.

2. Gently twist the stems from the mushroom caps. Set the caps aside and finely chop the stems.

3. Melt butter over medium heat. Sauté the mushroom stems, garlic, and green onions until tender. Add spinach and cook until the spinach is wilted and tender. Remove from heat and add remaining ingredients.

4. Stuff the mushroom caps with the mixture and place on the prepared baking sheet. Cook until the mushrooms are cooked through and the cheese is bubbly, about 8–10 minutes.

Serves 4–6

 **Quick and Easy**

●●●●●●●●●●●●●●●

TIP: Smooth, thin-skinned limes are the juiciest and least bitter.

SERVING SUGGESTION:
Serve with Latin- or Asian-influenced dishes.

Brazilian Lemonade

Hands-down both Sara and Kate's favorite drink. Ever. Don't be scared of sweetened condensed milk in this drink; we've yet to meet someone who doesn't love it!

1 cup sugar

6 cups cold water

4 juicy limes (see tip at left)

6 tablespoons sweetened condensed milk

1. Mix cold water and sugar very well and chill until ready to use. This step can be done ahead of time.

2. Wash limes thoroughly with soap (just use hand-dishwashing soap or regular hand soap); you need the soap to get the wax and pesticides off the limes because you're using the whole lime. Cut the ends off the limes and then cut each lime into eighths.

3. Place half of the limes in your blender. Add half of the sugar water, place the lid on your blender, and pulse 5 times.

4. Place a fine-mesh strainer over a pitcher (the one you'll serve the lemonade in) and pour the blended mixture through the strainer and into the pitcher. Use a spoon to press the rest of the liquid into the pitcher. Dump the pulp and residue in the strainer into the trash. Repeat with remaining limes and sugar water.

5. Whisk in sweetened condensed milk.

6. Serve immediately over lots of ice. This does not keep well, so while you can mix the sugar and water ahead of time and slice the limes, don't mix them in the blender until you are ready to serve.

Mango Coconut Smoothie

Mangoes are at their best and least expensive in the spring and summer months. Pick up a few of them when they're on sale for this sweet tropical treat.

1 cup cubed mango (about 1 medium mango)

⅓ cup cream of coconut (not coconut milk)

½ cup pineapple chunks, including some of the juice or syrup

Juice of one lime

Crushed ice

1. Combine chopped mango, cream of coconut, pineapple chunks and juice, and lime juice in blender. While blender is running, add crushed ice until desired consistency is reached.

2. Pour drink into glasses and garnish with additional mango, pineapple, maraschino cherries, or coconut as desired.

Tropical Punch

One sip of this drink will transport you to a faraway beach. It's perfect for tropical-themed parties and summer gatherings. You can freeze the leftovers and then allow the drink to partially thaw and blend it for a slushy treat.

Serves about 16

☆ Make Ahead
⊕ Quick and Easy

●●●●●●●●●●●●●●●●●

TIP: If you have leftovers, you can either freeze them or use your ice cream maker to blend this into a velvety smooth slush.

4 cups peach-mango juice (found with the refrigerated juices), divided

1 (15-ounce) can cream of coconut

5 cups pineapple juice

½ cup freshly squeezed lime juice (about 3–4 limes)

1 (1-liter) bottle of Sprite (or other lemon-lime soda)

1. Combine 3 cups of peach-mango juice with the can of cream of coconut in the blender. Blend until completely smooth.

2. Combine blended mixture with all other ingredients, except for the Sprite, in a serving bowl or pitcher. When ready to serve, add Sprite and serve over ice. Garnish with slices of lime, coconut, and/or pineapple if desired.

How to Cut a Mango

Mangoes have a big seed in the middle, so you have to cut around it. They're also super slippery when peeled, so you'll find it easier to cut first, peel second.

Mangoes are oval shaped, so you're going to cut off 2 wide sides and then 2 narrow sides. Hold the mango upright so that it is longer top to bottom than it is side to side, as in the picture. Start with a sharp paring knife at the top. Cut downward down one of the wide sides until you feel the seed. Just cut down the side, feeling the seed with your knife and cutting right around it.

Do the same with the opposite side. This is the majority of the fruit.

You'll now be left with the two narrow sides, so just cut around the seed to get those off too.

You can actually slice the large pieces while they are still in the skin and scoop them out like you would an avocado, or you can dice them the same way and just flip the skin inside-out so all the chunks pop out.

Serves 10–12

☆ **Make Ahead**

●●●●●●●●●●●●●●●●

VARIATION: Add a few spoonfuls of Strawberry Sauce (p. 71) to individual glasses for Strawberry Lemonade.

Fresh-Squeezed Lemonade

You can't beat fresh-squeezed lemonade on a hot summer day. For variation, try infusing it with fresh mint or basil from your garden.

2 cups sugar

8½–10½ cups water, divided

1 cup fresh lemon juice (about 5–6 large lemons)

¼ cup fresh lime juice

½ cup loosely packed fresh mint or basil leaves, optional

Ice cubes for serving

1. Combine sugar and 2½ cups water in a medium saucepan over medium heat. Stir until sugar has dissolved and then simmer 5 minutes. Remove from heat and cool about 20 minutes.

2. Add lemon and lime juices to sugar syrup. If not using mint or basil leaves, transfer to a covered pitcher and refrigerate. If using mint or basil leaves, place leaves in a covered pitcher or storage bowl. Pour lemon-lime mixture into container. Let stand one hour and then strain mixture and store until ready to serve.

3. When ready to serve, mix lemonade base with 6–8 cups cold water. Start with 6 cups and then adjust according to your taste. Six cups will be very sweet; 8 cups will border on watery. But however you like it, it will be delicious!

Caramel Apple Cider

You don't need expensive coffeehouse apple ciders when you can make this at home. Perfect for Halloween or other fall parties, especially to warm up after a night of trick-or-treating.

☆ **Make Ahead**

1 (64-ounce) bottle apple juice or cider

½ cup orange juice, freshly squeezed or a high-quality brand such as Simply Orange

2 cinnamon sticks

¼ teaspoon ground allspice

1 orange

8 cloves

⅓ cup bottled caramel sauce (plus more to taste if desired)

Sweetened whipped cream (p. 252 or from a can)

Ground cinnamon

TIP: The caramel sauce in this recipe will add a very mellow, sweet caramel flavor. For a more distinct caramel flavor, use a shot of caramel-flavored syrup. These sweet syrups are sold in bottles and can be found in the coffee aisle of the grocery store in a variety of flavors.

VARIATION: Substitute maple syrup for caramel sauce for a maple apple cider.

1. Pour the apple cider into a large stockpot on the stove. Set heat to medium-high. Add orange juice, cinnamon sticks, and allspice.

2. Thoroughly wash your orange and then gently stab the whole cloves into it. If you find it hard to do that without destroying the cloves, use a toothpick to poke little holes first and then insert the cloves.

3. Gently drop the whole orange into the pot. Bring the cider to a boil and then reduce heat to a low simmer. Simmer on low for 60 minutes or longer if you wish. If at any time the orange splits open, remove it from the pot.

4. After the cider has simmered for an hour, add caramel sauce and stir to combine and dissolve. Add more caramel to taste if needed.

5. When ready to serve, ladle the cider into mugs, top with whipped cream, and give it a drizzle of caramel and a sprinkle of cinnamon.

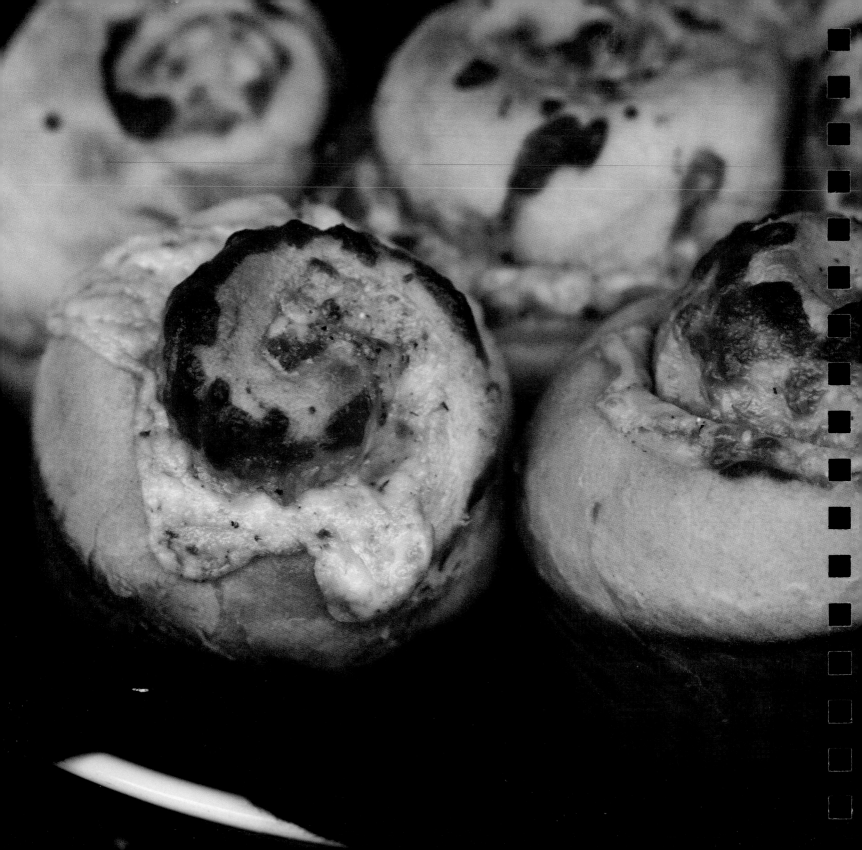

Breads

Facing page: Cheesy Garlic Bread Swirls, see page 33

Makes 12 breadsticks

Breadsticks

This recipe came from Kate and Sara's good friend, Lisa, and we believe it to have magical powers. Not only is this a great beginner recipe for yeast dough, but it will make you friends wherever you go.

1½ cups warm (105–115 degrees F.) water

1 tablespoon sugar

1 tablespoon active dry or bread machine yeast

½ teaspoon salt

3–4½ cups flour, divided

1. In a large bowl (the bowl of your mixer, if you have one), combine water, sugar, and yeast. Let stand for 10 minutes or until yeast is bubbly.

2. Add salt and stir. Add 1½ cups flour and mix well. Gradually add more flour (usually between 1½–2½ cups, depending on your elevation and your humidity) until dough starts to pull away from the sides of the bowl and it barely sticks to your finger.

3. Spray a glass or metal bowl with cooking spray and place dough in the bowl. Cover and let rise for 45 minutes or until doubled in bulk.

4. Remove from the bowl and place on a lightly floured surface. Spray a baking sheet with cooking spray. Roll dough into a rectangle 18 inches long and 9 inches wide and cut into 12 strips with a pizza cutter.

5. Roll out a piece of dough into a snake and then drape it over your forefinger and twist the dough. Place on baking sheet and repeat with remaining 11 pieces of dough. Try to space them evenly, but it's okay if they're close; pulling apart hot bread is one of life's greatest pleasures.

6. Cover the pan with a clean cloth and allow the dough to rise for another 30 minutes. When there's about 15 minutes to go, preheat your oven to 425 degrees F. When the dough is done rising, bake for 10–12 minutes or until golden brown. Rub some butter on top of the breadsticks (just put a zip-top bag on your hand, grab some softened butter, and rub it on the warm breadsticks) and sprinkle with Garlic Bread Seasoning (p. 53) or the powdery Parmesan cheese in a can and garlic salt. For a sweet treat, you can sprinkle the breadsticks with cinnamon sugar.

Homemade Pocket Sandwiches

Makes 8 sandwiches

1 recipe Breadstick Dough
Desired fillings: about 6–8 ounces of deli meat and 4–6 ounces of shredded cheese

1. Prepare dough through the first rise. After dough has risen the first time, turn it onto a lightly floured surface and roll into a rectangle 16 inches long and 8 inches wide. Using a pizza cutter, cut dough into 8 equal portions.

2. Leaving a little bit of a margin on the right and left sides, add toppings, with the cheese going on last. Stretch the dough out a little to give yourself a bit more dough to work with. Fold the left side over the middle and then the right side over that. Starting at the bottom of the "mummy," tightly roll the filled dough, stretching it very gently as you go to make sure you're getting a tight seal. Place on a sprayed cookie sheet and repeat with remaining dough.

3. When finished, cover the pan with a clean cloth and preheat your oven to 425 degrees F.

4. When oven has heated, bake pockets for about 15 minutes or until golden brown on top. For shine, you could brush the tops with a bit of egg white mixed with water during the last 5 minutes of baking, or you could rub a little butter on top of the rolls while they're still hot.

●●●●●●●●●●●●●●●●●

TIP: Rather than sprinkling your work surface with flour, you can always spray it with nonstick cooking spray for easy cleanup.

SERVING SUGGESTIONS:
Serve with any type of pasta dish or soup for a filling, comforting meal.

FREEZER INSTRUCTIONS:
After baking, freeze leftovers in a single layer and then place in a freezer-safe container. When ready to eat, wrap in a paper towel and defrost individual sandwiches in the microwave for 2–2½ minutes or until heated through.

●●●●●●●●●●●●●●●●

TIP: To get the water the right temperature, you don't have to measure it; just try and get water that would be comfortable for a hot shower, but not so hot that you wouldn't want to wash your face or hair in it.

SERVING SUGGESTIONS:
Slice a loaf of French bread in half, spread with mayonnaise, and fill with deli meats, cheeses, and sliced vegetables. Cut into 2-inch slices for sandwiches. You can also put any burger or sandwich on this bread.

French Bread, Hoagies, and Sandwich Rolls

This recipe for French bread is so easy and delicious that you'll make it whenever you need extra-tasty bread for sandwiches or for serving alongside soup, salad, or pasta.

1 tablespoon active dry or bread machine yeast

1½ cups warm water

1½ tablespoons sugar

1 teaspoon salt

3 tablespoons vegetable oil

1 egg, separated

4–5½ cups flour, divided

2 tablespoons cold water

1. Combine the yeast, water, and sugar in large mixing bowl and allow to stand 10 minutes or until bubbly.

2. Add salt, vegetable oil, and egg yolk (set the white aside for later) and combine. Add 3 cups flour and mix well until combined. Add enough remaining flour to make a soft dough that barely sticks to your finger. Knead, either by hand or in mixer for another 2–3 minutes. Cover and allow to rise 1 hour and 45 minutes (1½ hours will do in a pinch).

3. Punch down the dough. Spray a cookie sheet with nonstick cooking spray. For a loaf of bread, shape into a loaf and place on a greased cookie sheet. For buns or hoagies, divide equally into 8–10 (or even 12) pieces and shape as desired. Use a scale, if you have one, to get equal-sized buns.

4. It's okay if dough pieces touch (or will touch after having risen). Cover and allow to rise another 1¼–1½ hours or until doubled. Keep an eye on things—if they seem like they're getting so big that they might collapse, hurry and get them into the oven.

5. Preheat oven to 375 degrees F. Mix egg white with water and brush over dough. Bake for 10 minutes and repeat brushing the dough with the egg wash.

6. Bake an additional 8–10 minutes or until bread is golden brown and your house smells like heaven.

Cheesy Garlic Bread Swirls

Makes 12 rolls

Fresh, homemade bread, garlic butter, and melted mozzarella cheese—there's no way this recipe wouldn't be delicious!

1 recipe of French Bread dough (p. 32)

½ cup real butter, no substitutes

1½ tablespoons Garlic Bread Seasoning (p. 53)

1½ cups shredded mozzarella cheese

●●●●●●●●●●●●●●●●●

SERVING SUGGESTION:
Serve with any soup or Italian-themed dish.

1. Prepare the dough through the first rising step. Allow to rise 1 hour.

2. While the dough is rising, combine butter and garlic bread seasoning. Set aside.

3. When the dough has risen, roll the dough into an 18 x 6-inch rectangle on a work surface lightly sprayed with nonstick cooking spray or sprinkled with flour. Smear garlic butter over the entire surface of the dough and then sprinkle with cheese.

4. Roll up the dough jelly-roll style and then use dental floss to cut it into 12 equal slices. Place each slice in a muffin tin cup that has been sprayed with nonstick cooking spray. Cover with a clean cloth. Preheat oven to 350 degrees F. and allow rolls to rise while the oven is heating.

5. When the oven is ready, bake for 18–22 minutes. Be sure to keep a close eye on these during the last 10 minutes or so—once you notice the cheese getting brown, place a sheet of aluminum foil over the rolls (you don't need to press it down; just lay it on top). This will keep the cheese from burning. Although it will get pretty brown on top, the insides will still be perfectly melted.

•••••••••••••••••••

TIP: The fat in whole milk is absolutely essential to the lightness and flavor of these rolls. If you're in a pinch, 2% milk will work, but try to stay away from 1% or skim. If you're going to put all this work into these rolls, you want to make sure they taste amazing!

SERVING SUGGESTIONS:
These go with just about anything you can imagine. Or by themselves, slathered in Cinnamon Honey Butter (p. 51).

Dinner Rolls

These rolls are quite possibly the best we've ever had. Perfect for any major holiday (or sandwiches the next day), try making them one slow Sunday afternoon for a special treat and watch people come out of the woodwork.

2 cups whole milk (see tip)

½ cup plus 1 tablespoon sugar, divided

⅓ cup butter

2 teaspoons kosher salt

2 packages (4½ teaspoons) active dry or bread machine yeast

⅔ cup warm (105–115 degrees F.) water

8–9 cups all-purpose flour, divided

3 beaten eggs

1. Combine milk, ½ cup sugar, butter, and salt in a medium saucepan. Heat over medium heat until butter melts into salty-sweet perfection.

2. Remove from heat. Allow to cool to lukewarm. I usually rub some ice cubes along the sides of the pan or pop the entire pan in a sink full of ice cubes to cool the mixture down faster. This step is really important because if the mixture is too hot, it will kill the yeast.

3. While the milk mixture is cooling, dissolve the yeast and 1 tablespoon sugar in warm water. Let stand about 10 minutes. If the yeast hasn't bubbled, you'll need to repeat this step with new yeast.

4. In a large mixing bowl, combine 3 cups flour and milk mixture. Beat on low for 30 seconds, scraping sides of bowl constantly. Add yeast mixture and beat on high for 3 minutes. Add beaten eggs.

5. Stir in as much of the remaining flour as needed to make a soft dough. This dough should be very soft—it will be coming away from the sides of the bowl, but it will still stick to your finger when you touch it. Don't worry, it will firm up during the rising process. Part of what makes these rolls so good is that they're so soft and light; if you add too much flour, they will be heavy and dense. Place the bowl in a warm place and cover with a clean towel; allow to rise 1 hour.

6. Punch down dough. Lightly flour your work surface and turn dough out onto surface. Divide in half.

Spray two 9 x 13-inch glass pans with cooking spray. Roll first portion of dough into a rectangle and then cut it into 12 equal-sized pieces. We like to use a pizza cutter because it cuts right through dough without sticking to the blade. This dough should be very easy to work with, almost like Play-Doh. Shape each piece into a ball and place in prepared pan. Repeat with remaining dough in the second pan. Use a kitchen scale if you want to ensure that the rolls are exactly the same.

7. Cover with a clean cloth and allow to rise in a warm place for about 30 minutes. When dough has about 15–20 minutes to go, preheat oven to 375 degrees F.

8. Bake for 15–18 minutes or until golden brown.

9. When done, remove from oven. Rub a stick of cold butter over the tops of the rolls. Eat one now while it's still hot—that's your reward for making the world's best dinner rolls!

Herb-Rosemary Focaccia Loaves

Makes 2 loaves; serves 4–6

This bread tastes like something you'd find in an Italian restaurant. Instead of cutting it, just tear it with your fingers and dip pieces in extra-virgin olive oil drizzled with balsamic vinegar and seasoned with kosher salt and freshly ground black pepper.

● ● ● ● ● ● ● ● ● ● ● ● ● ●

SERVING SUGGESTIONS:
Serve with soups, salads, or any Italian-themed meal. It can also be sliced in half, layered with deli meats and cheese, and cut into party sandwiches.

1 cup warm (105–115 degrees F.) water

1 tablespoon active dry or bread machine yeast

1 tablespoon granulated sugar

2¼–2½ cups all-purpose flour, divided

1 teaspoon kosher salt, plus more for sprinkling

2 tablespoons rosemary (dried or fresh), divided

¼ teaspoon dried oregano leaves

¼ teaspoon garlic powder

2 tablespoons olive oil, divided

1. In a large mixing bowl, combine warm water, yeast, and sugar. Allow to stand for 10 minutes or until bubbly. While the yeast is getting bubbly, combine 2 cups of the flour, salt, 1½ tablespoons rosemary, oregano, and garlic powder in a medium bowl.

2. Add the flour mixture to yeast mixture along with 1 tablespoon olive oil. Mix well (I put it in my stand mixer fitted with the dough hook). Slowly add remaining flour to make a very soft, sticky dough.

3. Cover and allow to rise 45 minutes to 1 hour or until doubled.

4. Lightly flour your work surface or spray with nonstick cooking spray and transfer the dough onto this surface. Divide in half. Shape each half into a rounded loaf and place on a greased cookie sheet. Cover and allow to rise another 45 minutes.

5. Heat oven to 375 degrees F. Use remaining tablespoon of olive oil to brush over tops of loaves, discarding excess if you have any. Sprinkle with remaining rosemary and some kosher salt.

6. Bake for 15–20 minutes or until light golden brown. Serve immediately (if you can) with olive oil and balsamic vinegar.

Flour Tortillas

If you've never had or made homemade flour tortillas, you're in for a treat! They are so unbelievably easy and good that you'll never be able to go back to stale pre-packaged ones again!

⊙ **Quick and Easy**

2½ cups flour

¾ teaspoon kosher salt

¼ cup plus 2 tablespoons shortening

¾–1 cup hot water

1. In the bowl of a heavy-duty mixer fitted with the dough hook, combine the flour and salt. Add the shortening and combine until crumbly.

2. With the mixer running, slowly add ¾ cup of hot water. Mix until the dough starts to come together, adding more water if necessary; the dough should be about the consistency of Play-Doh.

3. Heat a large nonstick skillet over medium heat. While the pan is heating, divide the dough evenly into 8–10 balls. Roll the balls as thinly as possible into circles.

4. Place a raw tortilla onto the hot skillet and cook until large bubbles appear and the tortilla looks slightly oily, about 1 minute. Flip and cook another 30 seconds to a minute or until the tortilla is cooked through but not brown or burned. Repeat with remaining tortillas, keeping the cooked tortillas under a clean kitchen towel. Serve immediately if possible.

● ● ● ● ● ● ● ● ● ● ● ● ● ●

TIP: Rather than rolling out the tortillas individually, you can roll the dough out as thinly as possible into one large sheet and then use a bowl or a plate as a template to get perfectly round tortillas.

SERVING SUGGESTIONS: Serve with Grilled Taco Chicken (p. 114) or any other Mexican- or Latin-themed meal.

Makes 2 9-inch loaves

☆ **Make Ahead**

Almond Poppy Seed Bread

Try making this sweet quick bread in miniature bread pans to give as neighbor gifts during the holidays or as a "thank you" gift throughout the year. This bread is also great to serve at breakfasts and brunches.

3 cups flour

2½ cups sugar

1 teaspoon salt

1½ teaspoons baking powder

1½ cups milk

1⅓ cups vegetable oil

3 eggs

1½ teaspoons vanilla extract

1½ teaspoons almond extract

1½ tablespoons poppy seeds

Glaze

¾ cup powdered sugar

¼ cup orange juice

½ teaspoon vanilla extract

½ teaspoon almond extract

1. Preheat oven to 350 degrees F.

2. Whisk together the flour, sugar, salt, and baking powder. Add in milk, vegetable oil, eggs, extracts, and poppy seeds and beat for 1 minute. Pour batter into two 9-inch loaf pans sprayed with nonstick cooking spray. Bake for 50–60 minutes or until a skewer poked in the center comes out clean.

3. While the bread is baking, whisk the glaze ingredients together. When the bread is done, remove from the oven. Brush the glaze onto the hot bread and allow to cool.

Orange-Scented Zucchini Bread

Use some of the zucchini from your garden in this quick bread that's a perfect treat to make on a quiet fall afternoon.

2¼ cups flour

2 teaspoons cinnamon

⅛ teaspoon ground cloves

½ teaspoon salt

1½ teaspoons baking soda

3 eggs

½ cup canola oil

¾ cup granulated sugar

½ cup brown sugar

2 teaspoons vanilla

½ cup sour cream

Zest from one large orange

3 cups shredded zucchini

⅔ cup chopped pecans, toasted, optional

Topping

2 tablespoons granulated sugar

2 tablespoons brown sugar

½ teaspoon cinnamon

Makes 2 loaves

🌿 **Vegetarian**

ROLLOVERS
Zucchini
Pecans
Sour cream

●●●●●●●●●●●●●●●

TIP: When greasing and flouring pans for quick bread, grease and flour them all the way to the top and then use a paper towel to wipe about ½–1 inch off the top. This allows your bread to crown beautifully.

1. Preheat oven to 350 degrees F. Grease and flour 2 loaf pans and set aside.

2. Combine flour, cinnamon, cloves, salt, and baking soda in a bowl and whisk to combine. Set aside.

3. Beat eggs, oil, sugars, and vanilla for about 30 seconds. Add sour cream and orange zest and beat to combine. Mix in zucchini. Add dry ingredients and mix just until combined. Mix in pecans, if desired. Divide batter between 2 pans.

4. Combine topping ingredients and sprinkle evenly over top of loaves. Bake for 50–60 minutes or until a knife inserted in the center comes out clean.

5. Make sure to let your loaves rest on a cooling rack for at least 10 minutes before you try to remove them from the pan, or the bread will come out in chunks.

●●●●●●●●●●●●●●●●●

TIP: This recipe will make 2 very full 8-inch pans or slightly less full 9-inch pans, or you can bake one of each and the batter will fill each pan perfectly!

Chocolate Zucchini Bread

Zucchini adds moisture to this rich cake that has little bits of chocolate sprinkled throughout it. The cinnamon-sugary crust on top makes this a perfect treat to slip into a lunch box or snack on in the afternoon.

2 cups flour

2 teaspoons cinnamon

1½ teaspoons baking soda

½ teaspoon salt

¼ cup plus 2 tablespoons unsweetened cocoa powder

½ cup canola oil

1 cup granulated sugar

¼ cup brown sugar

3 eggs

2 teaspoons vanilla

½ cup sour cream

3 cups shredded zucchini

¾ cup mini chocolate chips

Topping

2 tablespoons brown sugar

2 tablespoons granulated sugar

½ teaspoon cinnamon

1. Preheat oven to 350 degrees F. Butter and flour 2 loaf pans and set aside. See tip at left for recommended pan sizes.

2. Mix topping ingredients in a small bowl and set aside.

3. Place flour, cinnamon, baking soda, salt, and cocoa powder in a small bowl and whisk to combine. Set aside.

4. With a stand or hand mixer beat oil, granulated sugar, brown sugar, and eggs until combined and slightly fluffy, 1–2 minutes.

5. Add vanilla and sour cream and mix until combined. Gently stir in the zucchini. Take a spoonful of the flour mixture and stir in with the chocolate chips (that will help keep them evenly distributed.) If you only have regular chocolate chips or a chocolate bar, just chop them so they're the size of mini chocolate chips. Stir remaining flour mixture into batter and mix just until combined. Add chocolate chips and stir to combine.

6. Divide the batter between the two pans and sprinkle topping over each.

7. Bake for 50–60 minutes. Set your timer for 45 minutes and then keep an eye on the loaves for the remaining time. When they're done, a toothpick or skewer should come out without goopy batter on it and the tops will be gorgeous and cracked with sugar. Remove from oven and let them cool on a rack for 5–10 minutes and then remove from pans. You definitely have to eat a slice warm—and slathered with butter.

☆ **Make Ahead**

ROLLOVER
Sour cream

●●●●●●●●●●●●●●●●

TIP: To quickly bring the eggs to room temperature, place them in lukewarm water for 10–15 minutes.

SERVING SUGGESTION: Use this as the base for Strawberry-Lime Shortcakes with Coconut Cream (p. 232).

Sour Cream Pound Cake

Sour cream adds moisture and flavor to this tender, versatile cake.

1½ cups flour	1 cup sugar
¼ teaspoon baking soda	3 eggs, room temperature
⅛ teaspoon salt	2 teaspoons vanilla
½ cup butter, softened	½ cup sour cream

1. Preheat oven to 350 degrees F.

2. In a small bowl, combine the flour, baking soda, and salt and set aside. Beat the butter and sugar until light and fluffy, about one minute. Continue beating and add eggs one at a time. Add the vanilla and sour cream. Slowly add the flour mixture while beating, and beat just until combined.

3. Pour the batter into a greased 8-inch or 9-inch loaf pan and bake for 50–60 minutes or until a skewer comes out clean. Cool for 10 minutes and then remove from pan.

Corn Bread

This isn't your dry, crumbly corn bread that you feel obligated to eat out of guilt—this is moist, cakelike, and something everyone will eat!

1 yellow cake mix

2 Jiffy corn bread mixes

Oil, milk, and eggs according to directions on both packages

1. Preheat oven according to directions on cake mix box. Combine cake mix and corn bread mixes in a large bowl. Add eggs, oil, and milk according to package directions (replace all water with milk). Mix together according to cake mix directions.

2. See tip at right about baking pans and then bake according to the times and temperatures on the cake mix box.

Makes 24 corn bread muffins

☆ **Make Ahead**

☽ **Quick and Easy**

🌿 **Vegetarian**

●●●●●●●●●●●●●●●●

TIP: This makes a lot of corn bread, but it's tricky to divide a cake mix well. However, you can bake this in one 9 x 13-inch pan plus one 8 x 8-inch pan and freeze the leftovers. It can also be baked in muffin tins.

SERVING SUGGESTIONS: Serve with Chipotle Chocolate Chili (p. 98) or with Honey Butter (p. 51).

Pico de Gallo, see page 48

Condiments, Spreads, and Garnishes

Facing page: Pico de Gallo, see page 48

Teriyaki Sauce

Makes 1½ cups

Sweet and savory, this quick and easy marinade comes together in minutes with ingredients you probably already have in your cupboard.

●●●●●●●●●●●●●●●●

SERVING SUGGESTIONS:
You can use this sauce as a marinade or to baste chicken or steak while grilling. It's also used in Teriyaki Chicken Salad (p. 83) as well as Bacon-Wrapped Teriyaki Chicken Skewers (p. 117).

½ cup granulated sugar

½ cup soy sauce

¼ cup cider vinegar

1 clove garlic, minced

½ teaspoon ground ginger

¼ teaspoon black pepper

1 tablespoon cornstarch

1 tablespoon cold water

1. Combine sugar, soy sauce, vinegar, garlic, ginger, and black pepper in a small saucepan. Bring to a boil over medium-high heat.

2. While the soy sauce mixture is heating, whisk together cornstarch and cold water. When the soy sauce mixture comes to a full boil, whisk in cornstarch mixture and stir sauce until thickened and clear. Remove from heat and allow to cool.

Fresh Basil Pesto

If you have basil growing in your garden, you'll probably reach a point where you won't know what to do with all of it! This pesto can be used immediately or frozen and stored for future use so you always have some on hand for a quick and easy meal or snack.

2½–3 cups basil leaves, gently packed

¾ cup freshly grated Parmesan cheese

3 garlic cloves, minced

⅓ cup pine nuts, toasted

½–¾ cup extra-virgin olive oil

Kosher salt, to taste

A few turns of freshly ground black pepper

1. Place all the ingredients except the olive oil in a food processor. For the salt, start with ¼ teaspoon and add the rest at the end. (The final amount really depends on the saltiness of your cheese, so give it a taste first.) Pulse the mixture a few times in the food processor.

2. Slowly pour in the olive oil while processor is running until you reach your desired consistency. Eat it right away or store in the fridge or freezer.

Serving size varies

☆ **Make Ahead**
☺ **Quick and Easy**
🌿 **Vegetarian**

●●●●●●●●●●●●●●●●

FREEZER INSTRUCTIONS:
Place pesto in ice-cube trays and freeze. When the pesto is frozen, transfer to a large zip-top bag.

SERVING SUGGESTIONS:
Serve on homemade pizza (p. 154 or 156) or over steamed veggies or baked potatoes. Mix it with mayonnaise for sandwiches, combine with cream cheese for bagels, or make Pesto Pasta (p. 170).

☆ **Make Ahead**
☉ **Quick and Easy**
🌿 **Vegetarian**

ROLLOVER
Fresh cilantro

●●●●●●●●●●●●●●●●

TIP: Although this tastes great the longer it stands, it might get a little soupy. If that's the case, just place it in a fine-mesh strainer and transfer back to a serving bowl.

SERVING SUGGESTION:
Serve with anything you would normally serve with salsa.

Pico de Gallo

You can make this fresh, addictive topping any time of year, but if you have garden-fresh tomatoes and jalapeños, you'll have to use some of them on this recipe! Kate's been known to forgo the chips and eat this with a spoon when no one's looking.

3 medium Roma tomatoes

½ small onion (white onions are traditional, but we love the color and flavor of red onions)

1 smallish jalapeño pepper

Juice of ½–1 lime, to taste

Approximately ¼ cup chopped cilantro

Kosher salt, to taste

1. Cut the ends off the tomatoes and then slice in half lengthwise. Under running water, gently run your finger under the membrane to remove the seeds; don't worry if a few seeds make it in. Cut the tomatoes into small chunks and place in a small mixing bowl.

2. Finely dice the onion. Toss with the tomato mixture.

3. Finely chop the jalapeño, removing the seeds if desired (the seeds contain the majority of the heat, although the flesh is still pretty hot). Toss with the tomatoes and onions.

4. Add the fresh-squeezed juice of half of the lime, stir to combine, and taste. Add a little more if desired.

5. Add the cilantro and mix well. Add a generous sprinkling of kosher salt, taste, and add more if desired. Refrigerate for 30 minutes if possible.

Garlic-Herb Sandwich Spread

Affectionately referred to as "magic mayo" by Sara's friends, this mayonnaise will make even the most basic turkey sandwich taste amazing. This is a great way to use up fresh herbs from your garden.

1½ cups mayonnaise

1 large clove garlic, minced or pressed

Zest from ½ lemon (¼ teaspoon)

1½ teaspoons fresh lemon juice

½ teaspoon fresh rosemary

1½ teaspoons fresh oregano

1 tablespoon fresh basil

1. Place the mayonnaise in a small food processor. Add minced garlic to the mayonnaise. Add lemon zest, then juice. Chop all herbs and add to mayo mixture.

2. Process until smooth and combined (or stir if doing by hand).

   This is best if made ahead so flavors have a chance to marry and intensify.

Makes 1½ cups

☆ **Make Ahead**

☉ **Quick and Easy**

ROLLOVERS
Fresh rosemary
Fresh oregano
Fresh basil

●●●●●●●●●●●●●●

SERVING SUGGESTIONS:
Serve on sandwiches, panini, or burgers.

Makes about 1½ cups

☆ **Make Ahead**
⊕ **Quick and Easy**

●●●●●●●●●●●●●●●●

TIP: If the guacamole gets an ugly brown skin on it, either skim the top off or just mix it in with the rest of the guacamole.

SERVING SUGGESTIONS:
Serve with Grilled Taco Chicken (p. 114), Chili-Lime Steak (p. 124), corn chips, or any Latin American-themed meal.

Guacamole

This guacamole is a perfect combination of creamy avocado, tangy lime juice, and flavorful garlic and onion. It's perfect for dipping tortilla chips or for putting on top of your favorite Mexican dish.

2–3 medium avocados, scooped from the skins (about 1¼ cup)

1 tablespoon fresh lime juice (about ½ of a lime)

½–1 teaspoon fresh minced garlic, to taste

2 tablespoons finely minced onion

¼ cup sour cream

Kosher salt, to taste

Pepper, to taste

3–4 tablespoons finely diced tomatoes, optional

Mash avocado with a fork in a small mixing bowl. Add remaining ingredients and combine well. Refrigerate in an airtight container. If possible, make about 30 minutes before serving to allow flavors to mingle.

Honey Butter

Warm homemade bread slathered with honey butter is a simple treat that's about as good as it gets. Try the cinnamon variation to mix things up a little.

Makes about 1½ cups

⏱ **Quick and Easy**

1 cup real butter

⅔ cup honey

¾ cup powdered sugar

1. Remove the butter from the refrigerator and allow to stand on the counter for about 20 minutes.
2. Place the butter in a medium mixing bowl. Add honey and powdered sugar and beat with an electric mixer for about 30 seconds or until everything is light and fluffy. Serve at room temperature.

●●●●●●●●●●●●●●●●

VARIATION: Add 1–2 teaspoons of cinnamon before you mix everything together.

SERVING SUGGESTIONS: Serve with warm Dinner Rolls (p. 34), Sopapillas (p. 68), warm Flour Tortillas (p. 37), or Corn Bread (p. 43).

How to Roast Garlic Cloves

If you've never tried roasted garlic, you definitely need to! Just pop a whole head in the oven and forget about it (except you won't be able to because your house will smell so heavenly).

Garlic	Kosher salt
Extra-virgin olive oil	Fresh cracked pepper

1. Preheat oven to 400 degrees F.

2. Using a whole head of garlic, peel off any excess paper around the edges. You want the cloves themselves to still be in their papers, but if you've got a lot of excess around the edges, just cut them off with kitchen shears.

3. Cut the top part off as in the picture at left, just enough to expose the cloves—approximately less than ⅓ of the head. Place the cut head on a piece of foil.

4. Sprinkle with a little kosher salt and pepper and drizzle with a couple of teaspoons of extra-virgin olive oil.

5. Tightly seal the edges of the foil around the garlic.

6. Place the wrapped garlic into the oven, directly onto the rack. If it's the only thing in your oven, bake at 400 degrees F. for about 30–40 minutes. You can also place it in the oven with something baking at a lower temperature; you'll just need to roast it for a bit longer.

7. Using a pot holder or a kitchen cloth, gently squeeze the wrapped garlic; when it's done, it should feel soft. When it's soft, remove it from the oven and let it cool for a minute.

8. The soft cloves will just slide out easily. You can either squeeze them out or use a fork to pop them out.

9. Use a fork to mash up the cloves into a paste. It adds a mild garlic flavor to so many things. It will keep for a week or more in your fridge in an airtight container. You can also freeze it and just grab a spoonful as you need it.

SERVING SUGGESTIONS: Spread directly onto baguette slices or mix with Oven-Roasted Tomatoes (p. 193). Add to mashed potatoes, cooked pasta, soups, sauces, mayonnaise, salad dressings, or bread dough just before kneading. Use in egg dishes or any other place where you want the sweet, mellow flavor of roasted garlic.

Garlic Bread Seasoning

You don't need to buy expensive garlic bread seasonings when you can easily make this at home for pennies. Store it in your fridge or freezer and then just pull it out when you need it.

½ cup powdered Parmesan cheese

2 teaspoons kosher salt

2 tablespoons garlic powder

2 teaspoons oregano

2 teaspoons basil

2 teaspoons marjoram

2 teaspoons parsley

Shake ingredients together in an airtight container. Store in the refrigerator for up to 3 months.

Makes about 1 cup

☆ **Make Ahead**
◔ **Quick and Easy**

●●●●●●●●●●●●●●●●

TIP: You might think you'll never use marjoram again, but we can pretty much guarantee that even if you buy it just for this recipe, you'll use it up in no time. In the meantime, store bulk herbs, or those you don't use often, in the freezer. To test if they're still good, open the lid and smell them. If you can't smell the herbs distinctly (or if you can't smell anything at all), toss them out and replace.

SERVING SUGGESTIONS:
Mix 1½ tablespoons of Garlic Bread Seasoning with ½ cup butter to spread on French bread or salmon. You can also sprinkle this over vegetables, baked potatoes, fish, or chicken.

Breakfast and Brunch

Syrups and Sauces

Facing page: Crêpes, see page 62

ROLLOVERS
Roasted red peppers
Green onions
Fresh cilantro
Flour tortillas

●●●●●●●●●●●●●●●●●

TIP: The egg mixture can be made a day ahead of time and stored in the fridge until ready to use.

FREEZER INSTRUCTIONS:
You can also store the taquitos by covering them tightly in plastic wrap and placing them in the fridge overnight, or freeze for later use. To prepare, place frozen taquitos directly on a baking sheet sprayed with nonstick spray. Follow original baking instructions, increasing time by 5 minutes or until the taquitos are golden brown.

SERVING SUGGESTION:
Serve with fresh fruit and juice for a crowd-pleasing breakfast.

Breakfast Taquitos with Lime-Chipotle Dip

Even the pickiest of eaters will eat these breakfast taquitos right up! You can heat up leftovers for quick weekday breakfasts that can be eaten in the car.

2 teaspoons extra-virgin olive oil

12 large eggs

½ cup sour cream

½ teaspoon kosher salt

¼ teaspoon freshly ground black pepper

½ teaspoon garlic powder

1½ cups shredded pepper jack cheese

¼ cup chopped roasted red bell peppers

¼ cup chopped green onions

¼ cup chopped cilantro

1–2 teaspoons hot sauce (like Tabasco or Cholula)

16 6-inch flour tortillas (see p. 37)

Cooking spray or olive oil

Dipping Sauce

1½ cups sour cream

1 tablespoon fresh lime juice

¼ teaspoon chipotle chili powder

½ teaspoon kosher salt

1. Preheat oven to 425 degrees F. Line a rimmed baking sheet with foil for easy cleanup. Spray with cooking spray or lightly brush with oil and set aside.

2. Heat olive oil in a large nonstick skillet over medium heat. Crack eggs into large mixing bowl. Whisk in sour cream, salt, pepper, and garlic powder. When the skillet is hot, add the egg mixture to pan. Using a rubber spatula, gently scrape bottom of pan and fold eggs over to scramble. Remove from heat when slightly undercooked. Add cheese, roasted red peppers, green onions, cilantro, and hot sauce to taste. Gently fold to combine.

3. Warm the tortillas in microwave to ease rolling process. Working with a few tortillas at a time, place a scant ¼ cup egg mixture into the center of each one and roll up into a cylinder. Place the rolled tortillas on the prepared baking sheet, seam-side down, so they are not touching each other.

4. When all tortillas are filled and rolled, lightly spray the tops with cooking spray or lightly brush with olive oil. Bake for 15 minutes or until edges are golden brown and crisp.

5. While the taquitos are baking, make the dipping sauce. Whisk together 1½ cups sour cream, lime juice, chipotle chili powder, and kosher salt. Cover and refrigerate. Remove the taquitos from the oven, allow to cool for 5 minutes, and then serve with the dipping sauce.

TIP: If you want to kick it up a little, use a 7-ounce can of chilies instead of a 4-ounce can and substitute ½ of the Colby Jack cheese with shredded pepper jack.

SERVING SUGGESTION:
Serve with fresh fruit and hot chocolate on Christmas morning.

Overnight Sausage and Egg Casserole

This casserole, which you make the night before and then pop in the oven in the morning, is Sara's family's Christmas morning tradition. Don't try and substitute whole wheat bread or low-fat cheese here.

6–8 slices white bread

About ¼ cup softened butter for buttering the bread

4 cups shredded Colby Jack cheese

12 ounces pork sausage, browned and drained if necessary

1 (4-ounce) can green chilies

6 eggs

2 cups milk

1 teaspoon kosher salt

½ teaspoon paprika

1 teaspoon oregano

½ teaspoon black pepper

¼ teaspoon garlic powder

¼ teaspoon dry mustard

1. Remove the crusts from your bread and lightly butter the bread slices on one side.

2. Place bread, buttered-side down, in a 9 x 13-inch baking dish. Six pieces of bread, plus 1 cut in half should cover the bottom of the pan with no big gaps.

3. Sprinkle shredded cheese evenly over the bread. Sprinkle the browned sausage on top of the cheese, and then top with the green chilies.

4. Whisk the eggs in a medium bowl. Add milk and seasonings and whisk to combine well.

5. Slowly stir the egg mixture while you pour it evenly on top of the assembled casserole. You'll want to keep stirring, or the spices will all gather in one spot and drop onto one single piece of casserole.

6. Cover well and place in the refrigerator overnight.

7. In the morning, preheat your oven to 350 degrees F. Bake for 50–60 minutes. The center should be set and the outside edges should be golden brown.

8. Allow the casserole to stand 10 minutes before serving. Don't worry if the casserole falls a little—that's completely normal.

Overnight Caramel Sticky Buns

Serves 8–10

☆ **Make Ahead**

No one will know this decadent yeast bread took fewer than 10 minutes to throw together. Prepare it right before you go to bed at night and pop it in the oven when you wake up in the morning.

18 Rhodes frozen dinner rolls

1 (4.6-ounce) box cook-and-serve pudding mix in either butterscotch or vanilla flavor

½ cup brown sugar

1 teaspoon cinnamon

½ cup pecans, optional

⅓ cup melted butter

1. Spray a Bundt pan with nonstick cooking spray. Place the frozen rolls evenly around pan. Sprinkle dry pudding mix, brown sugar, and cinnamon evenly over the top of rolls. Sprinkle with pecans, if desired. Pour melted butter evenly over everything. Cover with a clean dry towel and leave at room temperature overnight.

2. In the morning, preheat the oven to 350 degrees F. Bake rolls for 20–30 minutes or until golden brown. Let cool for 5 minutes and then invert onto a serving platter.

☆ **Make Ahead**
☉ **Quick and Easy**

ROLLOVERS
Spinach
Roasted red peppers
Green onions

●●●●●●●●●●●●●●●

TIP: When substituting liquid egg substitute for whole eggs, ¼ cup of egg substitute equals 1 whole egg.

FREEZER INSTRUCTIONS:
Store in an airtight container in the fridge, or freeze. If possible, remove from the freezer the night before to thaw in the fridge. When microwaving, set on a folded paper towel to absorb excess moisture.

SERVING SUGGESTIONS:
These can be eaten alone for a quick breakfast or served with a piece of whole wheat toast, fresh fruit, and a glass of milk.

Baked Ham and Egg Cups

Make these easily portable mini quiches ahead of time and then quickly heat them in the microwave in the morning for a fast, high-protein breakfast.

4 eggs

1 cup egg substitute or an additional 4 whole eggs

¾ cup shredded sharp cheddar cheese

¼ cup grated Parmesan cheese

¼ cup cottage cheese

5 ounces frozen spinach, defrosted, squeezed of water, and roughly chopped

⅓ cup diced roasted red peppers (bottled, or make your own, see p. 10)

1 ounce finely diced ham, Canadian bacon, or crumbled bacon (about ¼–⅓ cup)

¼ cup chopped green onions

¼ teaspoon kosher salt

⅛ teaspoon freshly ground black pepper

½ teaspoon hot sauce (like Tabasco or Cholula)

12 slices lunchmeat ham

1. Preheat oven to 350 degrees F.

2. In a bowl, combine all ingredients (except ham slices) and stir well.

3. Spray a muffin tin with nonstick cooking spray and place one piece of ham in each well to form a bowl.

4. Evenly divide the egg mixture between the 12 muffin wells (about ¼ cup each), being careful to keep ingredients evenly distributed. You want them to fill right up to the top.

5. Place in the preheated oven and bake for 15–20 minutes. The tops should be puffed and just barely set on top. Eggs will sink after cooling.

Makes 12–14 8-inch crêpes

☆ **Make Ahead**
◔ **Quick and Easy**
🌱 **Vegetarian**

●●●●●●●●●●●●●●●

TIP: Unfilled crêpes can be stacked between sheets of waxed paper and refrigerated or frozen. To thaw, leave at room temperature.

SERVING SUGGESTIONS:
Top sweet crêpes with Strawberry Sauce (p. 71), Buttermilk Caramel Syrup (p. 70), Hot Fudge Sauce (p. 252), or just a dusting of powdered sugar and sweetened whipped cream.

Crêpes

This is Sara's dad's famous breakfast tradition. In their house they call them "thin cakes" and eat them hot off the pan with butter and maple syrup. Whether they're sweet or savory, these are a delicious breakfast or dinner treat.

2 eggs

2 tablespoons canola oil

3 tablespoons sugar (omit if making savory crêpes)

1 cup flour

1⅓ cups milk

1. Combine all ingredients in a blender and blend on low speed until combined, or whisk by hand until there are no lumps.

2. Heat a nonstick skillet to medium-high heat. Hold the pan with one hand while you pour the batter with the other hand. Twirl the pan in a circular motion, pouring just enough batter to coat the bottom of the pan. Place on the heated cooking surface and cook until edges are set and you can easily run a rubber spatula around the edge of the pan, about 30 seconds. Flip crêpe and cook an additional 15–20 seconds. Remove crêpe from pan and either keep warm in the oven or cool to room temperature.

3. Fill with your choice of savory (meat, cheese, vegetable) or sweet (pudding, mousse, pastry cream, fruit) filling.

Double Chocolate Waffles with Berry Sauce

Makes 3–4 whole waffles or 12–16 quarters

Decadent, delicious breakfasts don't get much better than this! If chocolate for breakfast isn't your thing, try serving these as a base for vanilla ice cream with a drizzle of Buttermilk Caramel Syrup (p. 70) for dessert.

⅔ cup flour

⅓ cup cornstarch

¼ cup unsweetened cocoa powder

¾ teaspoon baking powder

¾ teaspoon baking soda

¼ teaspoon salt

⅛ teaspoon cinnamon

6 tablespoons granulated sugar

1 cup milk

⅓ cup vegetable oil

1 egg

1½ teaspoons vanilla

½ cup mini chocolate chips

Sweetened Whipped Cream (p. 252), for garnish

Cocoa powder, for garnish

Berry Sauce and Topping

¼ cup raspberry or strawberry jam

2 tablespoons hot water

3 cups berries, any combination, fresh or frozen

Powdered sugar, to taste, optional

●●●●●●●●●●●●●●●●

TIPS: Instead of pouring batter, use a ladle and spoon it onto the waffle iron, making sure to stir the batter each time so the chocolate chips will be evenly distributed. Also, leftover waffles can be frozen and heated in a toaster, toaster oven, or microwave for a quick breakfast.

1. To make the berry sauce, combine jam and hot water and whisk until combined. Gently stir in the berries until combined. Depending on the sweetness of the berries, you can add a little powdered sugar if you'd like. Set sauce aside.

2. Preheat waffle iron.

3. Whisk together flour, cornstarch, cocoa powder, baking powder, baking soda, salt, and cinnamon.

4. In a separate bowl, whisk together sugar, milk, oil, egg, and vanilla for about 1 minute or until it gets a little frothy.

5. Slowly add the wet ingredients into the dry ingredients a little at a time, whisking until just combined; be careful not to overmix. Stir in the chocolate chips. This is a pretty thin batter, so don't be expecting pancake batter.

6. You shouldn't have to grease your waffle iron. Ladle batter into waffle iron, being careful not to overfill. Bake according to the instructions for your waffle iron.

Puffed French Toast

●●●●●●●●●●●●●●●●

TIP: For dessert, top a warm piece of French toast with a scoop of vanilla ice cream.

VARIATION: Slice the bread into strips for great French toast dippers.

This is our ultimate French toast saved for special occasions—first days of school, birthdays, anniversaries. Try freezing the leftovers and then quickly heating them up on busy mornings!

2 eggs

2½ tablespoons sugar

½ teaspoon salt

½ teaspoon vanilla

2 cups milk

1 cup flour

2½ teaspoons baking powder

12 slices Texas-style toast, cut in half diagonally

Cinnamon Sugar

¾ cup sugar

1 tablespoon plus 1 teaspoon cinnamon

1. In a large skillet or frying pan, heat about ¼ inch of canola oil over medium heat. If you have a candy thermometer, you want to heat the oil to about 375 degrees F.

2. If you're not using a thermometer, test the oil heat by flicking some water into the frying pan. If it pops, reduce the heat. If hardly anything happens, turn up the heat. If it sizzles, it's just right.

3. While the oil is heating, whisk the eggs, sugar, salt, vanilla, milk, flour, and baking powder together in a shallow dish or pie plate.

4. Working quickly, take each half slice of bread and dip both sides in the mixture. Don't allow the bread to become too soaked in the batter. Gently shake the bread to remove excess batter and place in hot oil. Cook until puffed, golden brown, and a nice, crispy crust has formed on each side (probably 3–5 minutes per side; you really need to babysit them and make sure they're cooking correctly) and then remove from oil and drain on a paper towel. While cooking remaining French toast, keep cooked pieces warm in an oven set to the lowest temperature it will go.

5. When ready to serve, roll each piece in cinnamon sugar. If you're feeling really wild, drizzle the pieces of toast with a little maple syrup, Buttermilk Caramel Syrup (p. 70), Strawberry Sauce (p. 71), or try a pat of Honey Butter (p. 51).

Monkey Bread

No one will ever guess that these sweet, sticky bun bites started from refrigerated biscuits! Perfect for mornings when you want to serve something special but don't want to spend the time for homemade cinnamon rolls.

1 cup sugar

1 tablespoon cinnamon

3 (8-ounce) cans refrigerator biscuits, cut into fourths

½ cup butter

½ cup brown sugar

2 tablespoons honey

1. Preheat oven to 400 degrees F. Spray a Bundt pan with nonstick cooking spray and set aside.

2. Combine sugar and cinnamon in a large zip-top bag. Add the quartered biscuits, close the top, and shake to coat the biscuits in cinnamon sugar. Arrange in the prepared pan.

3. Place butter, brown sugar, and honey in a medium or large microwave-safe glass bowl or measuring cup. Cook on high for 1 minute at a time until the butter is melted and the ingredients can be easily mixed. Pour the mixture over the dough balls in the pan.

4. Bake for 20 minutes or until the bread is golden brown. Remove from oven and allow to stand for 5 minutes and then invert the pan onto a plate or serving platter.

Serves 10–12

⊕ **Quick and Easy**

●●●●●●●●●●●●●●●●●

TIP: Use a pair of kitchen shears to easily and quickly cut the biscuit dough.

Stuffed Apple-Cinnamon Rolls

This is a sweet version of our popular Stuffed Pizza Rolls (p. 164). These little bites are great as a dessert or a breakfast or brunch food.

1 package refrigerated pizza dough or 1 recipe Breadstick dough (p. 30)

Filling

2 cups shredded green apples (about 3 large apples)

3 tablespoons brown sugar

1 teaspoon ground cinnamon

1 tablespoon flour

Topping

1 tablespoon butter, melted

1 tablespoon sugar

¼ teaspoon ground cinnamon

Glaze

6 tablespoons powdered sugar

1 tablespoon melted butter

¼ teaspoon vanilla or almond extract

1–2 teaspoons milk

1. Preheat oven to temperature specified on pizza dough.

2. Spray a pie plate or similar dish with nonstick cooking spray and set aside.

3. On a lightly floured surface, roll the pizza dough into a rectangle approximately 12 x 18 inches. Using a pizza cutter, cut dough into 3-inch squares.

4. In a mixing bowl, combine the shredded apples, brown sugar, cinnamon, and flour. Divide evenly by putting a spoonful on each square of pizza dough. Use your fingers to close each square of dough, wrapping dough around filling and pinching to seal shut forming a round ball. Place balls seam-side down in pie plate.

5. Combine the topping ingredients and sprinkle on top of the dough. Bake for 15–20 minutes or until the rolls are golden brown on top. Remove from the oven and cool for 10 minutes.

6. While the rolls are cooling, whisk the glaze ingredients until smooth. Drizzle on top of the rolls and serve.

Makes about 24 small sopapillas

●●●●●●●●●●●●●●●●●

TIP: If you don't have a fryer, you can buy an inexpensive candy thermometer to measure the temperature of the oil.

VARIATION: Roll the dough into 8-inch circles and fry them. Top with Chipotle Chocolate Chili (p. 98), lettuce, chopped tomatoes, sliced olives, and sour cream for Navajo Tacos.

Sopapillas

These little fried pastries are kind of like doughnuts from South and Central America. They're often served with Honey Butter (p. 51), honey, or cinnamon sugar, but they can also be dusted with powdered sugar to make New Orleans-style beignets.

4 cups flour	4 tablespoons shortening
2 teaspoons baking powder	1½ cups warm water
1 teaspoon salt	1 quart of oil for frying

1. In a large bowl, mix flour, baking powder, salt, and shortening. Mix in water until smooth. Cover and let stand 30–40 minutes.

2. Roll out to ¼ inch thick. Cut into 3-inch squares. Heat oil to 375 degrees F. and fry until golden brown. Serve hot with cinnamon sugar or honey.

Apple Cider Syrup

Serve this warm, spiced syrup on a chilly fall morning over pancakes or French toast.

Makes 2½ cups

◷ **Quick and Easy**
☆ **Make Ahead**

2 cups apple juice

2 tablespoons lemon juice

2 tablespoons cornstarch

1 cup sugar

½ teaspoon cinnamon

¼ teaspoon nutmeg

½ teaspoon ground cloves

Combine all the ingredients and cook over medium heat just until thickened and clear. Refrigerate the leftovers for up to 1 week.

⊙ **Quick and Easy**

ROLLOVER
Buttermilk

●●●●●●●●●●●●●●●●

TIP: To measure sticky ingredients like corn syrup, honey, and molasses, spray the measuring cup with nonstick cooking spray first.

Buttermilk Caramel Syrup

One of our most popular recipes! Once you try this, you'll never go back to store-bought syrup! It's pretty much just like candy for breakfast. It's also amazing on desserts in place of caramel sauce.

¾ cup buttermilk

1½ cups sugar

½ cup real butter (no substitutions)

2 tablespoons corn syrup

1 teaspoon baking soda

1 teaspoon vanilla

1. Combine buttermilk, sugar, butter, corn syrup, and baking soda in a 4-quart pan.

2. Bring mixture to a boil and reduce heat to low—just make sure it's still bubbling. Cook, stirring very frequently, for 7–9 minutes or until the syrup reaches a rich golden brown. Remove from heat and stir in vanilla.

Strawberry Sauce

Make this in the spring when you can buy gorgeous, inexpensive strawberries and then freeze sauce to use all summer. Drizzle over ice cream, waffles, pancakes, cheesecake, or blend with vanilla ice cream and milk for strawberry milkshakes.

1 pint strawberries, washed, hulled, and roughly chopped

⅓ cup granulated sugar

1 teaspoon almond extract or vanilla

1. Combine berries, sugar, and vanilla in medium saucepan and bring to a simmer over medium heat. Cook for five minutes, stirring constantly and breaking strawberries up with a wooden spoon.

2. After five minutes, remove from heat and allow to cool before blending. When cool enough, transfer the mixture to blender and pulse until desired consistency is reached. Refrigerate unused sauce for up to 1 week or freeze for up to 3 months.

Makes about 2 cups of sauce

☆ **Make Ahead**
◔ **Quick and Easy**

●●●●●●●●●●●●●●●

TIP: Add a few spoonfuls to a glass of Fresh-Squeezed Lemonade (p. 26) for Strawberry Lemonade.

Salads

Salad Dressings

Facing page: Greek Couscous Salad, see page 79

☆ **Make Ahead**

🌿 **Vegetarian**

●●●●●●●●●●●●●●●●

TIP: When boiling eggs, use up the older ones in your fridge or buy them ahead of time and let them sit in your fridge for 1–2 weeks before boiling them; older eggs are easier to peel.

Potato Salad

No summer potluck or family barbecue is complete without a classic potato salad. This one adds smooth sour cream and bright herbs to round out the flavor.

3 pounds russet potatoes, peeled and cut into ¾-inch chunks

1 cup mayonnaise

⅓ cup sour cream

3 tablespoons vinegar or dill pickle juice

1½ teaspoons sugar

1½ teaspoons kosher salt

¼ teaspoon black pepper

2 tablespoons grated onion

½ teaspoon dried dill

1 teaspoon dried parsley

1½ cups diced celery

3 hard-boiled eggs

1. Place the potatoes in a large stockpot and cover with water. Bring to a boil and then reduce heat to a simmer. Cook potatoes 10–15 minutes or until fork-tender. Drain and cool to room temperature.

2. In a large mixing bowl, whisk together mayonnaise, sour cream, vinegar, sugar, salt, pepper, onion, dill, and parsley. Add potatoes and celery and stir to cover potatoes evenly with the dressing. Dice eggs and fold into potato mixture. Chill for at least 3 hours before serving.

Asian Cabbage Salad

This light, quick, and easy salad is a perfect way to recover your healthy eating habits after things get off track (and it tastes so great that you won't even mind!) Add some grilled chicken or shrimp for a more complete meal.

1 (14-ounce) bag coleslaw mix

1 rib celery, sliced

½ cucumber, sliced

About 20 sugar snap peas

½ red bell pepper, sliced

¼ small red onion, thinly sliced

1½ cups cooked, shredded or diced chicken, optional

1 tablespoon toasted sesame seeds (see tip on this page)

⅓ cup toasted slivered or sliced almonds (see tip on this page)

Dressing

2 tablespoons canola oil

2 tablespoons cider vinegar

¼ cup seasoned rice wine vinegar

2 tablespoons sugar (or equivalent sugar substitute)

1 teaspoon kosher salt

2 teaspoons soy sauce

¼ teaspoon garlic powder, or one small garlic clove, minced

¼ teaspoon freshly ground black pepper

½ teaspoon sesame oil

1. Make dressing first. Combine all ingredients in a sealed jar and shake extremely well. Store in the fridge until ready to use. This step can be done 2–3 days before serving the salad.

2. Place all salad ingredients, except sesame seeds and sliced almonds, in a bowl. Toss with dressing at least 30 minutes before serving. When you pour on the dressing, you might think it's not quite enough, but when it sits and marinates, it combines with the vegetables and draws out some of the liquid, so there will be plenty of dressing after it sits.

3. Refrigerate the salad for 30–60 minutes.

4. Right before serving, toss the salad with the toasted almonds and sesame seeds.

Makes 8–10 side dish servings and 4–6 main dish servings

☆ **Make Ahead**
☺ **Quick and Easy**
🦎 **Vegetarian**

ROLLOVERS
Cucumber
Red bell pepper
Red onion

●●●●●●●●●●●●●●●

TIP: To toast seeds and nuts, place them in a dry skillet over medium heat. Stir constantly until golden brown. Let cool before using. It's important not to toast more than one type together because of size differences and differences in the amount of oil in each type.

SERVING SUGGESTION:
Serve with chicken grilled in Teryaki Sauce (p. 46) for a healthy, Asian-inspired dinner.

Makes 8–10 side dish servings

⊙ **Quick and Easy**

ROLLOVERS
Spinach
Red onion

SERVING SUGGESTION:
Add grilled chicken to serve as a meal.

Spinach Mandarin Poppy Seed Salad

When Kate gets homesick for Utah, this is her favorite recipe to remind her of home. It's a great side dish and a big hit at parties, but it's also a delicious meal topped with sliced, grilled chicken breasts.

8 ounces (½ bag) baby spinach

½–1 head Romaine lettuce, chopped

½ thinly sliced medium red onion

1 large avocado, cubed

8 ounces mozzarella or Swiss cheese, shredded

1 (12-ounce) package bacon, cooked and crumbled

1 (12-ounce) can Mandarin oranges, drained

Poppy Seed Dressing (p. 90), to taste

Combine all ingredients except dressing in a large bowl. When ready to serve, toss with desired amount of salad dressing and serve immediately.

If you anticipate leftovers, just let your eaters dress their own salads because the dressing will make the greens wilt.

Barbecue Chicken Cobb Salad

A twist on the classic Cobb salad, using barbecue chicken adds a fun dimension of flavor and is a great way to use up leftovers.

12 cups Romaine lettuce

8–12 ounces grilled barbecue chicken

8 ounces bacon, cooked and crumbled

2 Roma tomatoes, seeded and diced

1 large avocado, pitted and diced

3 hard-boiled eggs, peeled and diced

⅓ cup sliced green onions

½ cup shredded cheddar cheese

Zesty Blue Cheese Dressing and Dip (p. 87)

Divide the lettuce among 4 plates. Top with chopped grilled barbecue chicken, bacon, tomatoes, avocado, hard-boiled egg, green onions, cheese, and blue cheese dressing. Serve immediately.

Serves 4

⊙ **Quick and Easy**

ROLLOVER
Green onions

TIP: If you don't like blue cheese dressing, add a few spoonfuls of your favorite barbecue sauce to ranch dressing.

Makes 10–12 side dish servings and 6–10 main dish servings

◷ **Quick and Easy**

🦜 **Vegetarian**

●●●●●●●●●●●●●●●●●

TIP: Day-old bread soaks up the vinaigrette more easily.

SERVING SUGGESTION:
Serve with grilled chicken or fish for a light, filling meal.

Panzanella

This traditional Italian bread salad is a great alternative to pasta or potato salads, especially for a fresh summer meal.

French bread or baguette loaves, cut into 1-inch cubes (you'll need 8 cups)

3 tablespoons olive oil

1 cucumber, peeled, seeded, and diced

1 yellow pepper, diced

4–5 large tomatoes, diced

1 small red onion, diced

1½ cups fresh mozzarella cheese cut into ½-inch cubes

⅓ cup chopped fresh basil

Vinaigrette

½ cup extra-virgin olive oil

2 tablespoons balsamic vinegar

2 tablespoons red wine vinegar

1 teaspoon Dijon mustard

1 clove garlic, pressed or finely minced

¼ teaspoon kosher salt

⅛ teaspoon black pepper

1. Preheat oven to 350 degrees F. Toss the bread cubes with 3 tablespoons olive oil and lay in a single layer on a baking sheet. Bake in preheated oven for 10 minutes. Remove from oven and cool to room temperature. This step is optional and isn't necessary if you don't want to heat up your house during the summer.

2. Combine the cucumber, yellow pepper, tomatoes, onion, mozzarella, and basil in a large bowl. Set aside.

3. Place the vinaigrette ingredients in a jar with a tight-fitting lid. Seal the jar and shake vigorously until combined. Pour over vegetables and add bread cubes. Combine well. Refrigerate for 15–20 minutes before serving, stirring periodically.

Greek Couscous Salad

If you've never tried couscous, it's a great alternative to rice or pasta, especially since it cooks in a matter of minutes. In this summery recipe, couscous is tossed with fresh garden vegetables and herbs, kalamata olives, tangy feta, and drizzled with a lemon-garlic vinaigrette.

1 (14.5-ounce) can chicken broth plus enough water to make 2 cups

½ teaspoon dry oregano leaves

1 teaspoon dry basil leaves

¼ teaspoon crushed dry rosemary

1 (10-ounce) box dry couscous (about 1½ cups)

2 cups diced tomatoes or 1 pint cherry or grape tomatoes, halved

1 medium cucumber, diced

½ cup diced red onion

½ cup kalamata olives, pitted and halved

½ cup crumbled feta cheese

½ cup chopped fresh parsley

Vinaigrette

½ cup extra-virgin olive oil

¼ cup fresh lemon juice

1 teaspoon lemon zest

1 tablespoon red wine vinegar

2 garlic cloves, pressed or finely minced

½ teaspoon kosher salt

¼ teaspoon freshly ground black pepper

Makes 8–10 side dish servings or 6 main dish servings

☆ **Make Ahead**

🌿 **Vegetarian**

ROLLOVERS
Red onion
Feta cheese
Fresh parsley

●●●●●●●●●●●●●●

SERVING SUGGESTION:
Add grilled chicken to make this a great meal all by itself.

1. Place the chicken broth and water, oregano, basil, and rosemary in a small pot on the stove top. Bring to a boil. Add the couscous, cover the pot with a lid, and remove from heat. Let sit for at least 5 minutes and then fluff with a fork. Cool to room temperature.

2. Combine cooled couscous, tomatoes, cucumber, onion, olives, feta, and parsley. Set aside.

3. In a small jar, combine vinaigrette ingredients and shake until combined. Pour over salad, stir, and then refrigerate 2 hours before serving. Season with additional salt and pepper to taste.

4. If desired, garnish with fresh parsley, extra feta cheese, and lemon slices for squeezing on top.

ROLLOVERS
Red bell pepper
Cucumbers
Red onion
Fresh cilantro

TIP: Spinach works great in this salad if you're serving it immediately, but if you're taking it to a potluck, stick with the Napa cabbage and romaine to keep things crunchy.

SERVING SUGGESTION:
Serve with Brazilian Lemonade (p. 22).

Thai Chicken and Noodle Salad

A rainbow of vegetables is tossed with cold noodles and crunchy, leafy greens before it's all tossed with a savory peanut dressing.

8 ounces linguine

4 cups shredded greens; any combo of Napa cabbage, romaine lettuce, or spinach

2 cups thinly sliced purple cabbage

½ red bell pepper, thinly sliced

½ yellow pepper, thinly sliced

1 medium carrot, julienned

½ medium cucumber, halved and sliced

¼ red onion, thinly sliced

3 cups diced grilled chicken

½ cup honey roasted peanuts (more if you want them)

1 recipe Thai Peanut Salad Dressing (below)

Thai Peanut Salad Dressing

½ cup creamy peanut butter

1 lime, juiced and zested

2½ teaspoons sesame oil

1 tablespoon seasoned rice wine vinegar

2 tablespoons soy sauce

3 tablespoons honey

2 cloves garlic, roughly chopped

1 tablespoon minced ginger

½ cup roughly chopped cilantro (stems and all)

¼ teaspoon kosher salt

2–3 teaspoons Sriracha chili sauce (start with 2 teaspoons and add more to taste)

½ cup vegetable oil

2–4 tablespoons water

1. Prepare dressing by combining all ingredients except oil and water in a blender. Blend for 20–30 seconds. Turn to low speed and slowly drizzle oil until combined. Add water to thin dressing to desired consistency.

2. Bring a large pot of salted water to a boil. Add pasta. While the pasta is cooking, chop the vegetables.

3. Drain pasta and run some cold water over it until it's cool. If not using it right away, add a drizzle of the salad dressing and stir to coat the noodles to prevent them from getting clumpy. Refrigerate until ready to use.

4. When you're ready to assemble the salad, place noodles, veggies, and chicken in a large bowl. Pour the Thai Peanut Dressing over everything, stirring as you go, until all ingredients are coated.

☆ **Make Ahead**

ROLLOVER
Green onions

●●●●●●●●●●●●●●●●●

TIP: Italian dressing makes a great all-purpose marinade for chicken.

Cranberry-Orange Chicken Salad

Tangy cranberries combine with green onions, crunchy celery, toasted nuts, and grilled chicken with a touch of fresh orange zest in this chicken salad that is perfect for dinner on a hot summer night or served at a baby or bridal shower.

1 pound chicken, marinated, grilled, and cut into small, bite-sized pieces (about 2 cups of chopped chicken)

1 cup celery, chopped

⅓ cup chopped green onions

Zest of 1 medium orange (about 1 tablespoon)

½ cup Craisins

½ cup mayonnaise

1 teaspoon coarse grain mustard

2 tablespoons jellied cranberry sauce

½ teaspoon kosher salt

¼ teaspoon freshly ground black pepper (or to taste)

½ cup chopped pecans, toasted

Croissants, rolls, or pita pockets

Lettuce leaves

1. In a medium bowl, combine chicken, celery, green onions, orange zest, and Craisins.

2. In a separate, smaller bowl, whisk together mayonnaise, mustard, cranberry sauce, salt, and black pepper. Add to the chicken mixture and toss to fully combine. This salad is best if refrigerated for several hours before serving.

3. Just before serving, add the toasted pecans. Serve on a croissant or roll with a crisp leaf of lettuce.

Teriyaki Chicken Salad

If classic chicken salad sandwiches aren't your thing, you might want to try these! Grilled teriyaki chicken is tossed with green onions and tropical fruits and a creamy teriyaki sauce. This recipe is perfect for a hot, summer night or a tropical-themed party.

2 chicken breasts

1½ cups Kikkoman Teriyaki Baste and Glaze or 1 recipe Teriyaki Sauce (p. 46)

2 stalks celery, finely chopped

⅓ cup sliced green onions, chopped

⅓–½ cup light mayonnaise

1 mango, cut into small cubes (or 1 [6-ounce] can of Mandarin oranges, drained)

1 (8-ounce) can pineapple tidbits or roughly chopped chunks

¼ cup sliced almonds, toasted

Salt and pepper to taste

Croissants or pitas

Lettuce leaves

1. Reserving about ⅔ cup of Teriyaki Sauce, marinate chicken in the remaining sauce for at least 4 hours. Grill chicken on medium heat for about 7 minutes per side, basting regularly with some of the reserved sauce.

2. While the chicken is grilling, combine the celery and green onions in a small mixing bowl or a plastic storage container with a lid.

3. When chicken is done, allow to stand for about 10 minutes and then cut into bite-sized pieces. Toss with celery and onions and then add mayonnaise and mix thoroughly. Start with ⅓ cup and go from there. Add 2–3 (or more) tablespoons of Teriyaki Sauce to taste. You want to add some of the great teriyaki flavor, but you also don't want it to be overwhelming. Refrigerate for at least 4–6 hours.

4. Just before serving, add mango (or oranges), pineapple, and nuts. Season with salt and pepper to taste. Serve with lettuce in a croissant or pita, or on a leaf of lettuce.

Serves 4–6

☆ **Make Ahead**

ROLLOVER
Green onions

●●●●●●●●●●●●●●●●

TIP: The thickness of the Kikkoman Baste and Glaze (or the homemade recipe) is important because it helps keep the dressing from becoming too runny.

SERVING SUGGESTION:
Serve with chunks of fresh watermelon (see p. 16).

☆ **Make Ahead**
🕐 **Quick and Easy**

ROLLOVER
Buttermilk

●●●●●●●●●●●●●●●●

TIP: If you don't have buttermilk, you can always combine 1 cup milk with 2 tablespoons vinegar or lemon juice and let the mixture stand for about 10 minutes.

SERVING SUGGESTIONS:
Serve on top of leafy greens or with Stuffed Pizza Rolls (p. 164), Oven-Baked Steak Fries (p. 182), or Breadsticks (p. 30).

Buttermilk Ranch Dressing

If you're suddenly out of ranch dressing, don't worry! This recipe comes together in just a few minutes and is made with stuff you probably already have in your kitchen, plus you don't have that chemical taste that's so prevalent in most store-bought ranch salad dressings.

1 cup mayonnaise (no substitutes)

⅔ cup buttermilk

¼ teaspoon white vinegar

1 teaspoon parsley

⅛ teaspoon dill

¼ teaspoon garlic powder

¼ teaspoon onion powder

1½ teaspoons dried chives

⅛ teaspoon black pepper

¼ teaspoon seasoned salt

⅛ teaspoon dry mustard

Whisk together the mayonnaise and buttermilk until the mixture is lump-free. Whisk in remaining ingredients. For best results, refrigerate for at least 4 hours before serving.

Creamy Cilantro-Lime Ranch Dressing

This recipe and the Cilantro-Lime Vinaigrette (p. 88) are recipes we developed to be similar to those at a very popular fresh-ingredient Mexican restaurant. If you don't love salads, these dressings can be used as marinades for chicken or fish or as dipping sauces for taquitos.

1 cup mayonnaise

½ cup milk or buttermilk

1 lime, juiced (about 2 tablespoons lime juice)

1 packet of Hidden Valley Ranch dressing mix (ignore the directions on the packet)

2 cloves garlic, roughly chopped

½ cup roughly chopped cilantro

¼ cup green salsa (La Costeña or Herdez brands are the most common)

Hot sauce (like Cholula or Tabasco), to taste

Combine mayonnaise, milk, lime juice, and the contents of the packet of ranch dressing in a blender. Add garlic, cilantro, and green salsa and blend to thoroughly mix all the ingredients. Season with hot sauce, if desired. If possible, refrigerate for several hours to allow the dressing to thicken and the flavors to meld.

Makes about 2 cups

☆ **Make Ahead**
⊕ **Quick and Easy**

ROLLOVER
Fresh cilantro

●●●●●●●●●●●●●●●

TIP: The heat level of store-bought green salsa varies by brand. Start with less than the recipe calls for and add more by taste.

SERVING SUGGESTIONS:
Drizzle over Chili-Lime Steak Salad (p. 124) or see the serving suggestion for the Cilantro-Lime Vinaigrette (p. 88).

Italian Dressing

This tangy dressing, made with easy-to-find ingredients you may already have in your house, is not only great on top of leafy greens but also works perfectly as a flavorful marinade for chicken, pork, or fish. Try it on grilled Italian Chicken and Vegetable Skewers, found on page 116.

●●●●●●●●●●●●●●●●●

TIP: When using oil in dressings and sauces, you can keep dressing from separating by emulsifying the oil into the rest of the ingredients, which just means blending the other ingredients and then slowly pouring the oil in while the blender or food processor is running. It can also be done by hand, but it's much harder to achieve good results with that method.

SERVING SUGGESTIONS:
Use as a marinade on chicken breasts, pork tenderloin, or a mild fish like tilapia before cooking on the grill.

¼ cup white, rice, or white wine vinegar

¼ cup lemon juice

2 teaspoons sugar

1 teaspoon dry mustard

½ teaspoon salt

½ teaspoon seasoning salt

½ teaspoon red pepper flakes (this really doesn't add much heat; it's better with it!)

¼ teaspoon black pepper

4 cloves garlic

1 cup canola oil

⅓ cup grated Parmesan cheese (either fresh or from a can)

¾ teaspoon Italian seasoning (add more if needed)

1. In a blender, combine vinegar, lemon juice, sugar, dry mustard, salt, seasoning salt, red pepper flakes, black pepper, and garlic.

2. While the blender is running, pour canola oil into the blender in a slow, steady stream (see tip on this page) until dressing is blended and the oil is incorporated into the dressing. Pour into a serving or storage container.

3. Whisk in Parmesan cheese and Italian seasoning. Refrigerate for at least 4 hours for the best flavor. Can be stored for up to 2 weeks.

Zesty Blue Cheese Dressing and Dip

Kate could probably eat this with a spoon, if that were considered appropriate in any way. The addition of red wine vinegar adds zip and tang to a dressing that might otherwise be considered old-fashioned.

1 cup mayonnaise (do not use Miracle Whip; however, light mayonnaise is a good alternative)

½ teaspoon kosher salt

½ teaspoon freshly ground black pepper

2 tablespoons red wine vinegar

2 teaspoons minced garlic (1–2 cloves)

½ cup crumbled blue cheese

1–2 tablespoons milk or buttermilk, optional

Whisk mayonnaise, salt, pepper, vinegar, and garlic together in a small bowl. Add in the blue cheese. If you prefer a thinner dressing, add a few table-spoons of milk or buttermilk until the desired consistency is reached. If possible, refrigerate for several hours before serving.

Makes about 1½ cups

☆ **Make Ahead**
☺ **Quick and Easy**

ROLLOVER
Blue cheese

TIP: If blue cheese is too strongly flavored for you, feel free to substitute feta cheese, which is milder.

SERVING SUGGESTIONS:
Serve with Stuffed Pizza Rolls variation (p. 164), Barbecue Chicken Cobb Salad (p. 77), or with your favorite vegetables.

●●●●●●●●●●●●●●

SERVING SUGGESTION:
Serve with Mexican-Style Sweet Shredded Pork (p. 140), homemade Flour Tortillas (p. 37), rinsed and drained black beans, Pico de Gallo (p. 48), and Crispy Corn Tortilla Strips (p. 141) for an amazing restaurant-like meal.

Cilantro-Lime Vinaigrette

This light and fresh Mexican-inspired vinaigrette is perfect on any green salad, especially in the heat of summer. It's also the perfect marinade for chicken breasts or white, flaky fish like tilapia or cod, making to-die-for fish tacos (especially when you drizzle a little more on top).

¼ cup fresh lime juice (about 2–3 juicy limes)

¼ cup white wine vinegar or rice vinegar

4–5 cloves garlic

½ teaspoon kosher or sea salt

2 teaspoons sugar

1 cup canola oil

½ cup roughly chopped cilantro, stems removed

1. In the jar of your blender, combine lime juice, vinegar, garlic, salt, and sugar. Blend until ingredients are completely combined.

2. With the blender running, add the oil in a steady stream. Add cilantro and blend until the cilantro has broken down but still maintains some of its texture. If possible, refrigerate at least 4 hours before serving. Serve with greens, on any type of Mexican salad, or use as a marinade.

☆ **Make Ahead**
⊙ **Quick and Easy**

ROLLOVER
Green onions

●●●●●●●●●●●●●●●●

SERVING SUGGESTION:
In addition to serving this on salad, you can make easy party sandwiches by spreading a few teaspoons onto sliced rolls (try our Dinner Rolls on p. 34) and then adding Swiss cheese and sliced ham. Close the sandwiches and place them on a baking sheet. Cover with foil and bake at 350 degrees F. or until the cheese is melted and the sandwiches are heated through.

Poppy Seed Dressing

This sweet and tangy dressing is the perfect complement for summer salads, sweet fruits, and smoky meats. Serve this on our Spinach Mandarin Poppy Seed Salad on p. 76.

⅓ cup white or white wine vinegar

1 teaspoon kosher salt

A few turns of freshly ground black pepper

¾ cup sugar

1 teaspoon prepared mustard

2 tablespoons sliced green onions

½ cup vegetable oil

1 teaspoon poppy seeds

1. In a blender, combine vinegar, salt, pepper, sugar, and mustard. While the blender is running, add the green onion. Continue running the blender and add the oil in a steady stream until it is fully incorporated into the dressing.

2. Pour the dressing into a serving or storage container and whisk in poppy seeds. Serve over leafy greens or on the Spinach Mandarin Poppy Seed Salad (p. 76).

Honey-Citrus Vinaigrette

This citrus-based vinaigrette also has a touch of honey, but it's not too sweet. It seems to be made for avocados and is perfect drizzled over our Spicy Honey Chicken Salad (p. 119).

Makes 1¼ cups

☆ **Make Ahead**
☉ **Quick and Easy**

1 garlic clove, minced

1½ teaspoons grated onion

⅓ cup fresh orange juice

3 tablespoons fresh lime juice

2 tablespoons honey

¾ teaspoon cumin

½ teaspoon salt

¼ teaspoon ground black pepper

⅓ cup vegetable oil

●●●●●●●●●●●●●●●
SERVING SUGGESTIONS:
Serve over Spicy Honey Chicken Salad (p. 119), drizzle over a platter of orange slices and sliced avocados, or just toss it with your favorite combination of salad greens.

Combine ingredients together in a jar and shake until well combined. Shake well before serving.

Soups and Chilis

Facing page: Chicken Tortilla Soup, see page 100

Black Bean Soup

●●●●●●●●●●●●●●●●

TIP: If you have an immersion blender, you can use that rather than placing the soup in the blender.

SERVING SUGGESTION:
Serve with a green salad tossed in Creamy Cilantro-Lime Ranch Dressing (p. 85) or Cilantro-Lime Vinaigrette (p. 88) and warm French Bread (p. 32).

This recipe takes Sara straight back to her mission in Brazil. It's rich and hearty but still healthy. Serve larger bowls with crusty bread and a tossed green salad or smaller cups alongside a half sandwich for an easy, satisfying meal.

1 tablespoon olive oil

¾ cup diced carrots (about 2 medium carrots)

¾ cup diced celery (about 1 rib)

1 cup diced onion (about 1 small-medium onion)

4 large cloves garlic, roughly chopped

2 (15-ounce) cans black beans, rinsed and drained

1 (3.5-ounce) can diced green chilies

2 (15-ounce) cans low-sodium beef broth

1 teaspoon kosher salt

⅛ teaspoon black pepper

½ teaspoon chili powder

¼ teaspoon cumin

½ teaspoon dry oregano leaves

1 bay leaf

1 lime, juiced, plus other limes, for garnish

Optional toppings: sour cream, tortilla chips, shredded cheese, chopped cilantro, etc.

1. Heat olive oil in a large stockpot over medium heat. Add carrots, celery, onion, and garlic and sauté for 4–5 minutes.

2. Add the black beans, chilies, and beef broth. Stir to combine and then add the salt, pepper, chili powder, cumin, oregano, and bay leaf. Simmer uncovered for about 20–25 minutes or until carrots are tender. Remove from heat. Remove bay leaf from soup.

3. Transfer the soup to a blender. Place lid on blender but remove the stopper in the lid to let heat escape. Cover the hole with a paper towel to avoid splatters.

4. Purée soup until desired consistency is reached. Squeeze in the juice from one lime and pulse to combine.

5. Ladle into bowls and top with desired toppings. Serve with extra lime wedges.

Cheddar-Broccoli Soup with Potatoes

This creamy, comforting recipe for cheddar-broccoli soup is unique because it doesn't use processed cheese in any form, but it's still rich, smooth, and flavorful.

Serves 6–8

🥒 **Vegetarian**

ROLLOVER
Cream cheese

●●●●●●●●●●●●●●●●
SERVING SUGGESTION: You can shape the dough for French Bread (p. 32) to make large bread bowls for serving.

1½ tablespoons butter

1 cup diced onion

4 cloves garlic, minced

2 (14.5-ounce) cans chicken broth

1 large baking potato, peeled and diced into ½-inch cubes

2 medium heads broccoli, chopped (about 4 cups florets and stems)

3 ounces cream cheese

2 cups low-fat milk

6 tablespoons flour

2 teaspoons kosher salt

¼ teaspoon freshly ground black pepper

4 cups shredded sharp cheddar cheese

3 tablespoons fresh or 1 tablespoon dried parsley

1. In a large stockpot, heat the butter over medium-high heat. When hot, add the diced onion. Sauté for 1 minute and then add garlic. Sauté 1–2 minutes longer or until onions are tender.

2. Add the chicken broth and potato and bring to a boil. Cover, reduce heat, and simmer for 10 minutes. Add the broccoli. Continue to simmer with the pot covered for about 5 more minutes or until both potatoes and broccoli are tender.

3. While the soup is simmering, combine cream cheese, milk, and flour in a blender and process until smooth. When potatoes and broccoli are tender, add the milk mixture to pot. Season with salt and pepper.

4. Simmer for about 5 minutes, stirring occasionally until thickened. Remove from heat and stir in cheddar cheese and parsley. If desired, use an immersion blender to blend until desired consistency is reached. You can also pulse it in a blender.

Vegetarian

ROLLOVERS
Cream cheese
Fresh basil

●●●●●●●●●●●●●●●●

SERVING SUGGESTIONS:
Serve with a warm panini or a grown-up grilled cheese sandwich made with Havarti and fresh basil.

Creamy Tomato Soup

This creamy, luxurious soup tastes and feels incredibly rich, but it's low fat! It's perfect with a toasted sandwich for chilly winter nights.

1 tablespoon reserved oil from sun-dried tomatoes or olive oil

1 cup chopped onion

¾ cup shredded carrot

4 cloves garlic, minced

⅔ cup sliced sun-dried tomatoes packed in oil

2 (14.5-ounce) cans diced tomatoes, undrained

1 (14-ounce) can chicken broth

1 teaspoon sugar

1 teaspoon kosher salt

¼ teaspoon freshly ground pepper

½ teaspoon dried oregano

1 tablespoon dried basil

½ teaspoon red pepper flakes, optional

3 ounces reduced-fat cream cheese

Garnishes: grated Parmesan cheese and fresh basil, optional

1. Place oil in a large saucepan over medium heat. Add onion, carrot, and garlic, and cook for 3–4 minutes or until vegetables are tender, stirring often.

2. Add sun-dried tomatoes, canned tomatoes, chicken broth, sugar, salt, pepper, oregano, and basil. If you're using red pepper flakes, add them now.

3. Bring soup to a boil and then reduce heat to simmer. Cover pan and simmer for 30 minutes.

4. Remove from heat. Transfer soup to a blender (do this in 2 batches if necessary). Add cream cheese. Remove center piece of blender lid to allow steam to escape, but place a paper towel over opening in blender lid to avoid splatters. Process for a few minutes until smooth. You could also add cream cheese directly to the pot and use an immersion blender to combine.

5. Add additional salt and pepper to taste and then divide soup among bowls. Garnish each serving with a sprinkle of grated Parmesan cheese and a fresh basil leaf if desired.

Creamy Corn Chowder

No one will ever guess this creamy rich soup is low in fat and calories! This deceptively rich soup is inexpensive, quick, easy, and filling.

Serves 4–6

⊕ **Quick and Easy**

6–8 ounces bacon (½ package)

2 tablespoons butter

¼ cup all-purpose flour

1 cup water

2½ cups 1% milk

2 chicken bouillon cubes or 2 teaspoons chicken base

2 red potatoes, diced into small cubes

¾ cup minced onion

2–3 cloves garlic, minced

1 (14-ounce) can corn, drained or about 1½ cups frozen fresh corn

A few dashes of hot sauce (like Tabasco or Cholula)

Salt and pepper to taste

Optional garnishes: extra crumbled bacon, shredded sharp cheddar cheese

●●●●●●●●●●●●●●●●●

TIP: Because different brands of bacon differ in their levels of saltiness, we haven't given a specific salt measurement. Taste as you go and be careful not to oversalt the soup.

SERVING SUGGESTIONS: Serve with a green salad, sweet Corn Bread (p. 43), or Breadsticks (p. 30).

1. Cook bacon until crisp.

2. While the bacon is cooking, melt the butter over low heat in a soup pot. When melted, add flour to make a roux and whisk until it comes together in a little ball. Add water and whisk until completely combined and there are no lumps. Add milk and chicken bouillon or base and bring to a simmer. Add potatoes, onion, and garlic, and simmer (but don't boil!), stirring very frequently, for about 20 minutes or until potatoes are tender.

3. Crumble the bacon and add to soup along with the corn. Heat through. Add a few drops of hot sauce and then salt to taste. Start with about ¼ teaspoon, give it a few minutes, and then add more if you need it.

4. Ladle into bowls and sprinkle with cheese and extra bacon if desired.

Chipotle Chocolate Chili

Don't be scared of chocolate in a chili recipe; it just adds richness and depth in a very short amount of cooking time. Like pretty much all great chili, this is even better the second day!

Serves 6–8

☆ **Make Ahead**

ROLLOVERS
Chipotle chilies
Green onions

● ● ● ● ● ● ● ● ● ● ● ● ● ●

TIP: To save unused chipotle chilies and sauce, purée the leftovers in a blender and then drop by teaspoonfuls onto a lined baking sheet. Place sheet in the freezer. When frozen, the chipotle chips can be stored in an airtight container in the freezer for 6 months.

SERVING SUGGESTION:
Serve with sweet Corn Bread (p. 43).

1–2 tablespoons olive oil

1 large onion, chopped

2–3 cloves garlic, minced

1 red bell pepper, chopped

1 pound lean ground turkey or beef

½ teaspoon kosher salt

½ teaspoon freshly ground black pepper

1 teaspoon ground cumin

2 tablespoons chili powder

3 tablespoons brown sugar

1 tablespoon unsweetened cocoa powder (not chocolate milk mix!)

2 (15-ounce) cans diced tomatoes

2 (14.5-ounce) cans kidney beans, drained and rinsed

1 (15-ounce) can beef broth

Chipotle sauce (from a 7-ounce can of chipotle chilies)

3–4 tablespoons red wine vinegar

½ ounce unsweetened chocolate (½ unsweetened baking cube), chopped (optional; use to taste as needed; be careful, because too much will make your chili bitter)

Chopped green onions, sour cream, or shredded sharp cheddar cheese, for garnish, optional

1. Heat olive oil in a large soup pot over medium heat. Sauté onion, garlic, bell pepper, and ground turkey or beef until meat is cooked through. Add salt, pepper, cumin, chili powder, brown sugar, unsweetened cocoa powder, tomatoes, beans, and beef broth. Add all of the chipotle sauce from a can of chipotle chilies. Heat to boiling and then reduce to a simmer (uncovered), stirring occasionally, until thickened as desired (about 30–40 minutes).

2. If desired, add some chopped chipotle chilies. Stir in 3 tablespoons red wine vinegar. Add chopped chocolate a small amount at a time until desired richness is reached. If necessary, add more red wine vinegar to cut the sweetness of the chili.

3. When thickened and seasoned as desired, serve with chopped onions or green onions, sour cream, and shredded cheddar cheese.

Serves 6–8

⊕ **Quick and Easy**

ROLLOVER
Fresh cilantro

●●●●●●●●●●●●●●●●●

TIP: Wear latex food-handling gloves when handling hot peppers, so that you don't transfer the oils via your hands to sensitive areas like your eyes and nose. To tell how spicy a jalapeño is, sniff it. The more it tickles your throat, the spicier it is.

Chicken Tortilla Soup

This tangy, chicken-based soup with tomatoes and a little kick from jalapeños tastes like it takes hours to make, but it's on your table in less than 30 minutes. This is a great go-to soup for family members or friends with wintertime colds.

1 recipe Grilled Taco Chicken (p. 114)

1–2 tablespoons olive oil

1 large onion, chopped

6 cloves of garlic, minced or pressed

1–2 jalapeño peppers, minced

4 (15-ounce) cans of chicken broth

1 (15-ounce) can chopped or diced tomatoes

¼ cup fresh lime juice (3–4 limes)

¼ cup chopped cilantro

1 teaspoon kosher salt

¼ teaspoon black pepper

Garnishes: crumbled Cotija or shredded pepper jack cheese, additional cilantro, lime wedges, and Crispy Corn Tortilla Strips (p. 141)

1. In a large stockpot, heat olive oil over medium heat. Add chopped onion and sauté for 3–4 minutes. Add garlic and jalapeño and cook a few minutes more until pepper is softened and garlic is fragrant. Add chicken broth and tomatoes and bring to a boil. Reduce heat and allow to simmer 15–20 minutes.

2. While soup is simmering, juice the limes and set aside. Start preparing the toppings: grate or crumble the cheese, chop the cilantro, cut up the avocado, and fry the tortillas. Right before serving, add lime juice, cilantro, and chopped chicken to the soup. Season with salt and pepper to taste. Ladle soup into bowls and add desired toppings.

Smoky Bean Soup with Ham and Bacon

Serves 4–6

This homemade version of the classic soup takes both of us back to our child-hoods when our dads would make us doctored-up Bean with Bacon soup. Smooth and creamy with a little smoke and garlic, this is comfort food at its best.

6 slices bacon (a few more if you want extra, for garnish)

1 cup diced onion (about 1 medium onion)

1½ tablespoons minced garlic (about 3 large cloves)

2 cups diced ham (about 10 ounces)

2 (15-ounce) cans Great Northern beans, drained and rinsed

1 teaspoon smoked paprika

½ teaspoon kosher salt

1 (32-ounce) box chicken broth

2 medium red potatoes, diced into bite-sized pieces (about 2–2½ cups)

½–¾ cup croutons, for garnish

TIP: Bacon grease shouldn't go down the drains in your sink, so after you cook the bacon, discard the grease into one of the empty bean cans.

SERVING SUGGESTIONS: Serve with panini or use up the rest of the bacon with a toasted BLT sandwich.

1. Cut the bacon into bite-sized pieces. Cook in a large stockpot until crisp. Remove bacon and drain on paper towels. Reserve 2–3 teaspoons bacon drippings in the pan and discard the rest.

2. Add the diced onion to the pan and sauté for about 2 minutes. Add the garlic and cook for an additional minute. Add the diced ham, beans, smoked paprika, and salt to pan and stir to combine. Then add the broth and the potatoes. Bring the soup to a boil and then reduce to a simmer.

3. Simmer for 10–15 minutes or until potatoes are tender. Remove from heat and stir in bacon. Use an immersion blender, if you have one, and blend until completely smooth.

4. If using a regular blender, ladle 3 cups of the soup into the jar. Place the lid on the jar, but vent the lid so the steam can escape.

5. Pour the blended soup back into the pot and stir to combine. Add additional salt and pepper if desired. Ladle into bowls and top with extra bacon and croutons if desired.

🍲 **Slow Cooker**

ROLLOVER
Fresh cilantro

●●●●●●●●●●●●●●●●●●

TIP: Leftovers for this recipe freeze really well. Place leftovers in 12-ounce disposable freezer-safe containers and freeze them as single servings for a quick and easy lunch.

SLOW COOKER INSTRUCTIONS: After cooking the chicken, transfer to the pot of a slow cooker and add remaining ingredients except for the lime juice, cilantro, and beans. Cook on low for 6–8 hours or on high for 3–4 hours. In the last 30 minutes, add lime juice, cilantro, and beans and cook until heated through.

FREEZER INSTRUCTIONS: After cooking the chicken, transfer the chicken mixture to a freezer-safe container and stir in remaining ingredients except for the beans, cilantro, and lime juice. Freeze for up to 3 months. When ready to cook, transfer to a slow cooker and cook on low for 7–9 hours or on high for 4–5 hours. In the last 30 minutes, add the beans, lime juice, and cilantro and cook until the beans are heated through. Serve with desired toppings.

White Chicken Chili

Tender chunks of chicken breast simmer with chilies, onions, garlic, and Mexican spices. Top with cilantro, sour cream, cheese, and chips for a perfect winter party food.

1 tablespoon extra-virgin olive oil

1 medium onion, diced (about 1 cup)

2 (15-ounce) cans Great Northern beans

1 pound boneless chicken, cubed (about 3–4 boneless, skinless breasts)

3–4 cloves garlic, minced

1 (3.5-ounce) can green chilies

½ teaspoon cumin

½ teaspoon dried oregano

½ teaspoon coriander

½ teaspoon salt

Freshly ground black pepper to taste

1 (32-ounce) box chicken broth

1 lime, juiced

½ cup chopped cilantro

Toppings: sour cream, chopped cilantro, shredded pepper jack or Monterey Jack cheese, avocado, tortilla chips (or make your own Crispy Corn Tortilla Strips on p. 141), lime wedges

1. Heat olive oil in a large pot over medium heat. Add the chopped onion and cook for about 2 minutes, just until it starts to become translucent.

2. While the onions are cooking, drain the beans and rinse with cold water; set aside. Sprinkle the chopped chicken with a little salt and pepper and add to pot. Add the garlic. Cook for 4–5 minutes or until there's no more visible pink on the chicken.

3. Add green chilies along with all of the juices in the can. Add the beans, cumin, oregano, coriander, salt, and a few turns of freshly ground black pepper. Stir to combine and then add the chicken broth.

4. Bring to a boil and reduce heat to a simmer. Simmer uncovered for 10–15 minutes. Remove from heat and add the juice from one lime and ½ cup of chopped cilantro. Add salt and pepper to taste.

5. Ladle into bowls and top as desired with sour cream, chopped cilantro, cheese, avocado, chips, or lime wedges.

🍲 **Slow Cooker**
🕐 **Quick and Easy**

ROLLOVERS
Fauxtisserie chicken
Fresh parsley

●●●●●●●●●●●●●●●●

TIP: Because of the dumplings or noodles, this soup does not store well. If you have leftovers, try removing the noodles or dumplings before refrigerating, as they will absorb the liquid from the soup.

VARIATION: Instead of dumplings, use 1 (8-ounce) package of Kluski noodles. Cook with the soup until noodles are tender.

SERVING SUGGESTIONS:
Serve with Breadsticks (p. 30), a loaf of homemade French Bread (p. 32), or a batch of Dinner Rolls (p. 34).

SLOW COOKER INSTRUCTIONS: Combine all ingredients except for the evaporated milk and the dumplings or noodles and cook on low for 6–8 hours or on high for 3–4 hours or until the carrots are tender. Turn heat to high and add noodles or dumplings and continue cooking until the dumplings or noodles are cooked through.

Chicken and Dumplings

Chicken and dumplings is a yummy Southern-inspired twist on the ultimate comfort food, chicken noodle soup.

1–2 tablespoons olive oil

1 onion, minced

2–3 cloves garlic, minced or pressed

6 cups chicken broth

1 pound cooked chicken, cut into bite-sized pieces (about half a Fauxtisserie Chicken, p. 110)

1 bay leaf

½ teaspoon basil

1 cup sliced carrots

2 ribs celery, chopped

1 handful of chopped fresh parsley (or 1 tablespoon dried parsley)

1 (12-ounce) can evaporated milk, optional (fat-free is fine)

1 recipe Bisquik biscuit dough

1. In a large pot, heat some olive oil over medium heat and add onion and garlic. Sauté for 2–3 minutes and then add chicken broth, chicken, bay leaf, and basil. Bring to a boil.

2. Add carrots and celery and reduce heat to a simmer. Cover and cook until carrots and celery are tender. When carrots and celery are almost done, add chopped parsley. Stir in evaporated milk. Increase heat to boiling and drop Bisquik dough by the spoonful into the boiling soup. Cover and cook until the dumplings have cooked through.

Italian Meatball Soup

Flavorful, bite-sized Italian meatballs are simmered in a tomato and chicken broth soup with garlic, onion, and Italian herbs. You can definitely serve this crowd-pleasing soup for company.

1 recipe of Italian Meatballs (p. 163)

1–2 tablespoons olive oil

1 onion chopped

4–5 cloves of garlic, minced

5 (14-ounce) cans chicken broth

1 cup water

1 (28-ounce) can crushed tomatoes

1 tablespoon Italian seasoning

2 carrots, peeled and diced

1 cup small pasta (like macaroni), uncooked

2 cups spinach, thinly sliced

1. When preparing the meatballs, make them small and bite-sized. Broil the meatballs according to the recipe directions until they are just brown and can maintain their shape.

2. While the meatballs are cooking, heat 1–2 tablespoons olive oil in a large stockpot. Sauté the onions and garlic until translucent. Add broth, water, tomatoes, and Italian seasoning. Heat to boiling. Gently add the meatballs, carrots, pasta, and spinach. Reduce heat to a simmer and cook for 10 minutes or until the meatballs are cooked through, the carrots are tender, and the pasta is al dente.

Serves 8–10

ROLLOVER
Spinach

●●●●●●●●●●●●●●●●

SERVING SUGGESTIONS:
Serve with Breadsticks (p. 30), Cheesy Garlic Bread Swirls (p. 33), or a loaf of homemade French Bread (p. 32).

FREEZER INSTRUCTIONS:
After cooking the meatballs, garlic, and onions, transfer them to a large freezer-safe container. Add the chicken broth, tomatoes, spinach, carrots, and Italian seasoning. Freeze for up to 3 months. When ready to serve, transfer to a slow cooker and add 1 cup water. Cook on low for 8–10 hours or on high for 6–8 hours. Right before serving, cook the pasta separately on the stove top until al dente, drain, and add to the soup.

Meats

Facing page: Italian Chicken and Vegetable Skewers, see page 116

Baked Creamy Chicken Taquitos

It's pretty rare for reduced-calorie alternatives to traditionally fried foods to taste as satisfying as the original, but these are an exception. The creamy filling is quick to throw together and can be made ahead of time. The tortillas bake up so crispy and flavorful that you won't miss the deep-fried calories for even a second! This is definitely one of the most popular recipes with our readers.

Makes 14–16 corn tortillas or 10–12 flour tortillas

☆ **Make Ahead**
🌿 **Vegetarian (variation)**

ROLLOVERS
Fauxtisserie chicken
Cilantro

SERVING SUGGESTION: Try dipping in Creamy Cilantro-Lime Ranch Dressing (p. 85).

FREEZER INSTRUCTIONS:
Place unbaked taquitos in a single layer on a baking sheet and place in the freezer for 2 hours or until frozen enough to hold their shape. Pack in a freezer-safe container for up to 3 months. To bake, follow the regular instructions, extending the baking time by 10 minutes.

MAKE AHEAD: To make dinnertime assembly a breeze, prepare this filling up to 2 days ahead of time and store in the fridge in an airtight container.

⅓ cup (3 ounces) cream cheese

¼ cup green salsa

1 tablespoon fresh lime juice

½ teaspoon cumin

1 teaspoon chili powder

½ teaspoon onion powder

¼ teaspoon granulated garlic

3 tablespoons chopped cilantro

2 tablespoons chopped green onions

2 cups cooked, shredded chicken

1 cup shredded pepper jack cheese

6-inch corn or flour tortillas (as fresh as possible; the longer they sit, the more likely they are to crack)

2 tablespoons vegetable oil, optional

Nonstick cooking spray

Kosher salt

---

1. Heat oven to 425 degrees F. Line a baking sheet with aluminum foil and spray it lightly with cooking spray.

2. Heat cream cheese in the microwave for 20–30 seconds so it's soft and easy to stir. Add green salsa, lime juice, cumin, chili powder, onion powder, and granulated garlic. Stir to combine and then add cilantro, green onions, chicken, and pepper jack cheese.

3. Wrap 3–4 tortillas at a time in damp paper towels and microwave for 20–30 seconds so they are soft and pliable. If you find your tortillas are cracking when rolled, use damper paper towels and increase the microwave time.

4. Place 2–3 tablespoons of the chicken mixture on the lower third of each tortilla, keeping it about ½ inch from the edges, and then roll it up.

5. Place seam-side down on the baking sheet in a single layer. Spray the tops lightly with cooking spray or brush with vegetable oil. Sprinkle with a pinch of kosher salt on top. Place pan in the oven and bake for 15–20 minutes or until crisp and the ends start to get golden brown. Cool for 5–10 minutes and then serve with sour cream, Guacamole (found on

p. 50), Quick and Easy Salsa (p. 12), or Pico de Gallo (p. 48). Makes approximately 16 taquitos.

Vegetarian Black Bean Taquitos

1 (14-ounce) can black beans, rinsed and drained

2 tablespoons bottled salsa

1 garlic clove, minced

½ teaspoon cumin

½ teaspoon kosher salt

¼ teaspoon freshly ground black pepper

2 tablespoons fresh lime juice

1 (10-ounce) box frozen spinach, thawed, drained, and roughly chopped

¾ cup frozen corn kernels

½ cup diced roasted red peppers

1 cup shredded cheese (Monterey Jack, pepper jack, or cheddar)

8–10 soft-taco-sized whole wheat tortillas

1. Preheat oven to 425 degrees F.

2. Place ¾ cup of the beans in a food processor with the salsa, garlic, cumin, salt, pepper, and lime juice. Process until mostly smooth. Transfer the mixture to a medium bowl and add remaining ingredients (except the tortillas), including the rest of the beans. Mix together.

3. Place about ¼ cup of the bean mixture on each tortilla. Roll up the tortillas and spray with nonstick cooking spray. Bake in preheated oven for 20–25 minutes or until edges are golden brown and crisp. Serve with Creamy Cilantro-Lime Ranch Dressing (p. 85) for dipping.

Fauxtisserie Chicken

Slow-roasting a whole chicken in a slow cooker yields moist, tender meat without a fuss. Fresh herbs, spices, and vegetables make endless options for variations. Serve part of the chicken for dinner one night and save the remainder for another meal such as Baked Creamy Chicken Taquitos (p. 108), White Chicken Chili (p. 102), or Teriyaki Chicken Salad (p. 83) later in the week.

Serves 4–6

🍲 Slow Cooker

●●●●●●●●●●●●●●●●

SERVING SUGGESTION:
Serve with Roasted Garlic-Rosemary Potatoes (p. 181) and a green salad for an easy-yet-fancy dinner.

1 (3 ½–4 pound) whole chicken

1 teaspoon seasoning salt

4–5 whole cloves of garlic, peeled

Optional: fresh herbs, such as rosemary, oregano, sage, basil, or tarragon. See variations.

1. Make 3 balls of aluminum foil about 2 inches in diameter. Place them in a triangular pattern on the bottom of your slow cooker. These balls hold the chicken off the bottom of the dish so the hot air can circulate all around the chicken and so the chicken isn't stewing in its own juices.

2. Slice garlic cloves lengthwise into thin slices and set aside.

3. Rinse chicken in cold water. Make sure to include the cavity and remove and discard any chicken parts inside the cavity. Pat dry with paper towels.

4. Place the chicken on a plate so it lies with the breast facing up and the legs on the plate. Loosen the skin of the entire chicken and gently separate the skin from the bird while keeping it attached around the edges. Use your hands to place the sliced garlic cloves under the skin.

5. Rub seasoning salt onto the skin of the chicken. Place chicken breast-up on the foil in the slow cooker. Cover with the lid, turn heat to low, and cook for 6–7 hours or until a meat thermometer inserted into the thickest part of the breast registers 160 degrees F.

Classic Roasted Bird

4 tablespoons softened butter

4 cloves minced garlic

2 tablespoons chopped parsley

1 teaspoon dried sage

1 onion

2 carrots

Combine butter, garlic, parsley, and sage. Use fingers to spread mixture underneath the chicken skin and lightly around the outside of the chicken. Peel one onion and cut into quarters. Peel 2 carrots and cut into 2-inch pieces. Distribute onions and carrots inside the cavity and around the outside of the chicken.

Cajun

Cajun seasonings, salt-based, such as Tony Chachere's or Emeril Essence

In place of the seasoning salt, use Cajun seasoning. Add an additional 2–3 cloves of garlic under the skin as well.

Chili-Lime

2–3 tablespoons chopped cilantro

1½ teaspoons chili powder

1 teaspoon cumin

1 lime

Spread cilantro under the skin with the garlic called for in the main recipe. Add chili powder and cumin to the seasoning salt mixture. Cut one lime in half and rub both halves all over the outside of the chicken. Place lime halves inside the chicken cavity before cooking.

Lemon-Rosemary

Few sprigs of fresh rosemary

1 lemon

Place sprigs of rosemary under the skin of the chicken. Cut one lemon in half and rub juices all over the outside of the chicken before applying the seasoning salt. Place both lemon halves inside the chicken cavity before cooking.

Chicken Cordon Bleu

You might be surprised how easy it is to make this classic at home. Panko bread crumbs help keep the chicken crispy on the outside and tender on the inside.

3 boneless, skinless chicken breasts

½ teaspoon garlic powder

½ teaspoon onion powder

½ teaspoon seasoned salt

¼ teaspoon black pepper

1 cup shredded mozzarella, provolone, or Swiss cheese

6–12 slices thinly sliced ham

½ cup all-purpose flour

2 eggs, lightly beaten

1 cup panko bread crumbs

½ cup freshly shredded Parmesan cheese

1½ tablespoons butter, melted

1. Preheat oven to 350 degrees F. Spray a baking sheet with nonstick cooking spray.

2. Place a breast on a cutting board and place your non-dominant hand on top of it. Using a sharp knife, cut each breast completely in half horizontally. Place each piece between two pieces of plastic wrap and, using a meat mallet, pound until the piece is about ¼ to ½-inch thick. Repeat with remaining breast halves; you should have 6 pieces of chicken.

3. Combine seasonings and sprinkle evenly over one side of each chicken piece. Divide shredded cheese among all pieces, layering on top of the spices. On top of the cheese, layer 1–2 pieces of ham. Roll each chicken piece up and secure with toothpicks.

4. Place flour in a shallow bowl, eggs in another bowl, and both panko bread crumbs and Parmesan cheese in a third, stirring to combine.

5. Working with one piece of chicken at a time, dredge in flour, rolling the chicken around to cover the whole piece, then in eggs, and finally in bread crumb mixture. Use your fingers to press bread crumb mixture in on all sides of chicken.

6. Place chicken on prepared baking sheet. Drizzle melted butter evenly over chicken. Bake for about 25–35 minutes or until internal temperature reaches 165 degrees F. If desired, place pan under the broiler to lightly brown the tops of the chicken.

7. Cool for 10 minutes before serving. Remove toothpicks.

Crispy Coconut Chicken Fingers

Makes 12 tenders; serves 4–6

Who didn't love chicken fingers growing up? Your kids will think you're making it for them, but really, the flavors are all grown up. Even though they're baked rather than fried, the panko bread crumbs and coconut add plenty of crunch while the chicken remains tender. Bottom line? Everyone will love these.

1 cup sweetened coconut flakes

1 cup panko bread crumbs

1½ teaspoons garlic powder

¾ teaspoon table salt

¾ teaspoon curry powder

¼ teaspoon onion powder

⅛ teaspoon cayenne pepper, optional (it doesn't add a lot of heat, but kids might be sensitive to it)

½ cup flour

2 eggs

12 chicken tenders (you may use more or less depending on their size)

●●●●●●●●●●●●●●●

TIP: Whisk together 1 cup apricot-pineapple preserves, 2 teaspoons soy sauce, ½ teaspoon Dijon mustard and ⅛ teaspoon curry for a great dipping sauce.

SERVING SUGGESTIONS:
For gourmet fast food at home, serve with Oven-Baked Steak Fries (p. 182) and Fresh-Squeezed Lemonade (p. 26). Or replace the Spicy Honey Chicken with these leftover chicken tenders in the salad on p. 119.

1. Preheat oven to 450 degrees F. Spray a foil-lined baking sheet with non-stick cooking spray and set aside.

2. Chop coconut so it's roughly the same size as the bread crumbs.

3. Combine the coconut, bread crumbs, and spices in a shallow dish. Stir well to make sure everything is evenly distributed.

4. Place the flour in a shallow dish and the eggs in another shallow dish. Whisk the eggs.

5. Working with one chicken tender at a time, dredge the chicken in flour, shaking off any excess. Then dip in the egg, again shaking off any excess. Roll in the bread crumb/coconut mixture, gently pressing the mixture onto the chicken. Place on the prepared baking sheet. Repeat with remaining chicken tenders. To add a little extra crunch, you can drizzle each one with a tiny bit of olive oil, but it's completely optional.

6. Bake for about 20 minutes or until juices run clear, being careful not to overcook them. If the tenders are smaller, the time might be closer to 15 minutes, whereas if you have larger tenders, it could be closer to 25 minutes, so keep a close eye on them. Either way, the coconut and bread crumbs will be lightly golden brown and crispy.

●●●●●●●●●●●●●●●●

TIP: Do not use chicken tenderloins because they will become dry and their smaller size throws off the spice-to-meat ratio.

SERVING SUGGESTION:
Serve with homemade Flour Tortillas (p. 37), Pico de Gallo (p. 48), Guacamole (p. 50), and shredded cabbage (just use a packaged coleslaw mix without the dressing), and crumbled Cotija cheese for a fun, fresh, Mexican dinner.

Grilled Taco Chicken

No one will ever guess this amazing-tasting chicken is so simple to make. Use it to fill taco shells or tortillas for tacos or burritos or on top of chopped Romaine lettuce for a healthy lunch.

1 pound boneless, skinless chicken breasts

2–3 juicy limes

1–2 tablespoons red wine vinegar

3 cloves garlic, minced or pressed

1 teaspoon chili powder

½ teaspoon cumin

½ teaspoon kosher salt

½ teaspoon freshly ground black pepper

1. Place chicken breasts in a heavy-duty zip-top plastic bag.

2. Squeeze limes over chicken. Add splash of vinegar and the minced garlic. Seal the bag and shake to distribute the marinade. Marinate for 4–8 hours.

3. Preheat grill to medium-high heat (about 400 degrees F.).

4. Combine chili powder, cumin, salt, and pepper in a small bowl. Remove chicken from bag and discard the used marinade. Rub the spices into the chicken.

5. Place chicken breasts on the hot grill. Grill for 7 minutes, turn, and grill for an additional 5–7 minutes (5 minutes for smaller chicken breasts, no longer than 7 minutes for larger ones). Remove from heat to a clean plate and allow to stand for 5 minutes before slicing and serving.

How to Peel Garlic

To easily peel garlic, lay a clove of garlic onto your work surface. Place the broad side of your knife against the garlic and then carefully (but firmly) smash the knife with the heel of your hand. The paper on the garlic should slide right off. You can also smash the garlic with a heavy glass and then peel the paper off.

Italian Chicken and Vegetable Skewers

High-quality bottled Italian dressing like Bernstein's works great in this recipe, but our easy, homemade Italian Dressing (p. 86) makes these skewers really amazing. There's nothing like cooking vegetables on the grill to bring out fabulous flavor in mushrooms, zucchini, and red bell peppers.

●●●●●●●●●●●●●●●●●

TIP: When using bamboo skewers on the grill, soak them in a pan of water for at least 30 minutes so they don't burn while the food is cooking on the grill.

SERVING SUGGESTION:
Perfect for a meal on a warm summer night served with cubed watermelon (p. 16) and Fresh-Squeezed Lemonade (p. 26).

1 pound boneless, skinless chicken breasts, cut into bite-sized pieces

1 recipe of Italian Dressing (p. 86), or 1 bottle of high-quality dressing like Bernstein's or Newman's Own, divided

1 each medium green and yellow zucchini, cut into ½-inch slices (and halved if the zucchini is thick)

1 yellow, red, or orange bell pepper, cut into bite-sized pieces

1 small red onion, carefully cut into bite-sized chunks. Try to keep as much of the onion intact as possible, but don't worry if it the pieces start coming apart.

Sweet cherry or grape tomatoes

8 ounces white mushrooms, washed and stems removed

1. Place cut-up chicken in a shallow dish and pour about ½ of the dressing over the chicken. Cover, refrigerate, and marinate for 2–3 hours.

2. Gently toss the vegetables in the remaining dressing. Set aside.

3. If using bamboo skewers, see the tip on this page. Thread meat and vegetables onto the skewers keeping in mind that you'll have far more vegetables than chicken; you'll probably have around 3 pieces of chicken per skewer but as many veggies as you can fit.

4. Preheat grill to medium-high heat or around 400 degrees F. Cook skewers, turning at least once, for 10–12 minutes or until chicken is cooked through and the veggies are tender-crisp.

Bacon-Wrapped Teriyaki Chicken Skewers

These bacon-wrapped bites of teriyaki-marinated chicken are guaranteed to please just about everyone. For a meal, thread them onto a skewer or just use a toothpick to serve them as an appetizer.

8 ounces bacon (not thick-sliced)

1 pound boneless, skinless chicken breasts

1 (16-ounce) can pineapple chunks

1 recipe Teriyaki Sauce (p. 46)

1. Cut the bacon into thirds. Count how many pieces you have and then keep that in mind when cutting up the chicken breasts.

2. Cut the chicken into bite-sized pieces; you'll want roughly as many pieces of chicken as you have of bacon.

3. Drain the pineapple and place in a bowl or on a plate to avoid cutting your hand by reaching into the can repeatedly. Set up a workstation with toothpicks or kabob skewers, chicken, bacon, and pineapple, plus a shallow dish or heavy-duty zip-top plastic bag for marinating the skewers.

4. Wrap a piece of bacon around a piece of chicken and secure with a toothpick. If making larger skewers, thread the meat all the way to the bottom. Top with a chunk of pineapple. For skewers, repeat twice so there are three pieces of bacon-wrapped chicken on the skewer. Repeat with remaining chicken, bacon, and pineapple.

5. Reserve ½ cup of Teriyaki Sauce and pour the remaining sauce over the chicken. Marinate for 4–8 hours.

6. If you choose to cook these on the grill, preheat the grill to medium-high heat (about 400 degrees F.). Place skewers on grill and baste with reserved Teriyaki Sauce. Cook for 7 minutes, turn, baste, and cook for another 7 minutes.

7. To cook these in the oven, preheat oven to 400 degrees F. and place on a foil-lined baking sheet. Cook for 20 minutes, turning and basting once.

Makes 8–10 skewers or 24–30 appetizers

☆ **Make Ahead**

●●●●●●●●●●●●●●●

TIPS: To keep the bite-sized skewers warm at a party, pop them in a slow cooker set to low heat. For using bamboo skewers, see tip on facing page.

SERVING SUGGESTION: Serve with Lime-Cilantro Rice with Pineapple (p. 204), Caramelized Green Beans (p. 188), and Brazilian Lemonade (p. 22).

Orange Chicken with Snow Peas

Serves 4–6

☺ **Quick and Easy**

ROLLOVER
Fresh ginger

●●●●●●●●●●●●●●●●

TIP: To de-string snow peas, snip the tough ends off the pea pod and find the string that runs the length of the pod. Gently pull it off and discard it. Some peas will have stronger, more visible strings than others, so if you have a hard time finding the string, don't worry about it because you probably won't notice it when you're eating it, either.

Takeout from Asian restaurants is one of the most popular weekend activities, but it can be pretty harsh on your waistline and your wallet! Try this healthier homemade Orange Chicken recipe that you can customize to your own tastes. Want to kick up the heat a little? Add some extra red pepper flakes!

2 teaspoons vegetable oil

3 cloves garlic, minced

2 teaspoons minced ginger or bottled minced ginger

1½ pounds boneless, skinless chicken breasts cut into 1-inch pieces

½ teaspoon kosher salt

¼ teaspoon black pepper

2 tablespoons cornstarch

⅓ cup orange juice

½ cup orange marmalade

2 tablespoons soy sauce

1½ tablespoons brown sugar

3 tablespoons rice wine vinegar

⅛ teaspoon red pepper flakes

8 ounces fresh snow peas, trimmed of the string (see tip)

Hot white rice for serving

Sesame seeds, optional

1. Heat vegetable oil in a large skillet or wok set to medium heat. Add minced garlic and ginger and sauté for 30 seconds. Sprinkle chicken with salt and pepper and add to pan. Stir-fry until chicken is cooked through, about 5 minutes.

2. While chicken is cooking, whisk together cornstarch and orange juice in a bowl. Whisk in marmalade, soy sauce, brown sugar, vinegar, and red pepper flakes and set aside.

3. Add snow peas to chicken and cook for about 1 minute. Add sauce to pan and increase heat if needed to bring to a simmer. Cook for about 3–4 minutes or until sauce is thickened. Serve over white rice and sprinkle with sesame seeds if desired.

Spicy Honey Chicken

One of the most popular recipes on our blog, this sweet and slightly spicy chicken works great by itself or served in a salad with creamy avocados, sweet mangos, red onions, and a to-die-for citrus-based vinaigrette.

8 boneless, skinless chicken thighs (thighs work better in this recipe than breasts); about 2 pounds

2 teaspoons vegetable oil

Glaze
½ cup honey

1 tablespoon cider vinegar

Rub
2 teaspoons granulated garlic

2 teaspoons chili powder

½ teaspoon onion powder

½ teaspoon coriander

1 teaspoon kosher salt

1 teaspoon cumin

½ teaspoon chipotle chili powder

1. Preheat grill to medium-high heat or about 400 degrees F.

2. Combine rub ingredients in a small bowl.

3. Trim any visible fat off the chicken thighs, rinse, and pat dry with a paper towel. Drizzle oil over chicken and rub it in with your hands. Rub the spice rub into the chicken thighs. Grill for 3–5 minutes on each side.

4. For the glaze: while chicken is cooking, warm honey in the microwave for about 15 seconds. Whisk in vinegar. Reserve 2 tablespoons glaze and brush the rest on the chicken in the final moments of cooking. Remove chicken from the grill and allow to stand 3–5 minutes. Drizzle reserved 2 tablespoons of glaze over the chicken while it's standing.

Serves 4–6

🕐 **Quick and Easy**

●●●●●●●●●●●●●●●

SERVING SUGGESTIONS:
Serve chicken in the salad (below) or alongside Sweet and Savory Coconut Rice (p. 203) and asparagus grilled with olive oil, garlic, kosher salt, and pepper.

Spicy Honey Chicken Salad

Makes 4 large salads or 6 smaller salads

1–2 heads Romaine or red leaf lettuce

2 ripe mangoes, chilled

2–3 ripe avocados

1 small red onion, sliced

1 recipe Honey-Citrus Vinaigrette (p. 91)

While chicken is grilling, wash lettuce and divide among plates. Slice mangos, avocados, and onions and arrange on top of lettuce. When chicken has rested for 5 minutes after cooking, slice and divide among the salad plates. Serve immediately with Honey-Citrus Vinaigrette.

⊙ **Quick and Easy**

ROLLOVER
Sour cream

●●●●●●●●●●●●●●●●

SERVING SUGGESTION:
Serve with any green vegetable or a tossed salad.

Beef Stroganoff

Comfort food casual enough for a weeknight dinner but sophisticated enough for company.

1 pound top sirloin or tenderloin steak

½ teaspoon kosher salt

¼ teaspoon black pepper

3 tablespoons butter, divided

8 ounces sliced mushrooms (like creminis)

¾ cup diced onion (about 1 small onion)

4 cloves garlic, minced

¾ cup warm water

1 teaspoon beef bouillon granules, beef base, or one bouillon cube

2 tablespoons flour

2 teaspoons Worcestershire sauce

½ cup sour cream

1. Slice steak into strips ¼-inch thick and about 2 inches long. Sprinkle with salt and pepper and set aside.

2. Melt 2 tablespoons butter in a large skillet over medium heat and then add mushrooms, onion, and garlic to pan. Sauté for 4–5 minutes or until mushrooms are browned and onions are tender. Remove mushrooms, onions, and garlic from pan and set aside.

3. Slightly increase the heat and melt 1 tablespoon of butter in pan. Add beef and sauté, stirring, for 3–5 minutes or until pink is no longer visible.

4. While the beef is cooking, whisk water, bouillon, flour, and Worcestershire sauce together until smooth. Add this mixture to the beef and return the mushroom mixture to the pan as well. Bring the sauce to a simmer and cook for 1–2 minutes to thicken. Remove pan from heat and stir in sour cream. Add additional salt and black pepper to taste. Serve over egg noodles or white rice.

Orange Thai Beef Skewers

Thin slices of steak are marinated in a spicy, savory mixture with a hint of orange and grilled for just a few minutes until the beef is tender.

1 orange (zest and juice)

¼ cup soy sauce

¼ cup seasoned rice wine vinegar

1 tablespoon honey

1 tablespoon sesame oil

1 teaspoon ground ginger

1 teaspoon coriander

4 cloves garlic, minced

2–4 teaspoons Sriracha chili sauce (start with 2 teaspoons and add more to taste)

1½ pounds flank steak

●●●●●●●●●●●●●●●●

TIP: When using bamboo skewers, soak them for at least 30 minutes in a pan of water to prevent them from burning. Metal skewers are a great alternative if you don't want to bother soaking the bamboo skewers.

SERVING SUGGESTION:
Serve Sweet and Savory Coconut Rice (p. 203) and fresh-cut fruit.

1. Zest the entire orange into a bowl. Cut the orange in half and juice the orange; add the orange juice to the zest.

2. Whisk the soy sauce, vinegar, honey, sesame oil, ginger, coriander, and garlic into the orange juice and zest. Add Sriracha to taste.

3. Slice the steak against the grain into ¼-inch slices. Place the steak slices into a zip-top bag and pour the marinade over the steak. Refrigerate for 4–8 hours.

4. Preheat grill. Thread the pieces of steak onto skewers (see the tip for using bamboo skewers). Grill over medium-high heat for 3–4 minutes and serve immediately because these cool quickly.

☆ **Make Ahead**

ROLLOVERS
Queso fresco or Cotija cheese
Chipotle chilies with adobo sauce

●●●●●●●●●●●●●●●

TIP 1: When working with chipotle peppers, wear rubber, latex, or plastic food-server gloves to protect your skin from both burning and discoloration.

TIP 2: A great way to warm your corn tortillas is to heat a large cast-iron skillet over medium-high heat and have a bowl of water ready next to the stove. When the skillet is hot, spray the skillet with nonstick cooking spray and dip 2–3 tortillas at a time in the water. Place on the skillet and steam them until they become light brown and fragrant, or about 1 minute. Flip the tortillas and cook for another 30–60 seconds. Keep warm under a moistened paper towel.

SERVING SUGGESTIONS:
Serve with Guacamole (p. 50), Pico de Gallo (p. 48), and Quick and Easy Black Beans (p. 202), or Lime-Cilantro Rice with Pineapple (p. 204).

Chipotle Beef Taquitos

Tender, shredded beef is combined with seasonings and smoky chipotle peppers and then rolled in white corn tortillas with tangy queso fresco and lime and baked until crisp rather than fried. The best part? All the ingredients can roll over from other meals, cutting down on your workload.

3 cups cooked, shredded beef roast (similar to the beef from the Slow Cooker French Dip Sandwiches on p. 134)

¼–½ teaspoon minced chipotle pepper in adobo sauce (¼ teaspoon is mild)

1 (4-ounce) can green chilies, undrained

1 tablespoon adobo sauce from the canned chipotle peppers*

1 teaspoon garlic powder

1 teaspoon coriander

½ teaspoon cumin

1 teaspoon chili powder

Zest from 1 lime

1 tablespoon fresh lime juice

1 package queso fresco or Cotija cheese, crumbled (about 12 ounces)

About 20 6-inch white corn tortillas

Olive oil or cooking spray

1½ teaspoons kosher salt

*If you don't want to work with the chipotle peppers or can't find them, try adding some chipotle chili powder. You can find it by the other spices in the grocery store. It will still give you a smoky spice, so start with a little and increase according to taste.

1. Preheat oven to 425 degrees F.

2. Slice the shredded beef against the grain into pieces about ½ inch to 1 inch long. Place in a bowl and set aside.

3. Working carefully, remove 1 chipotle pepper from the can, trying to leave as much sauce in the can as possible (see Tip 1 for more information on working with chipotle peppers). Slit the pepper open and scrape out the seeds. Mince the pepper and use as much as needed.

4. Combine chilies, chipotle pepper, adobo sauce, garlic powder, coriander, cumin, chili powder, and lime zest and juice in a bowl. After stirring to combine, gently toss together with shredded beef.

5. Wrap a pile of about 10 tortillas in damp paper towels and microwave for 1 minute to soften. Repeat with remaining 10 tortillas. Or you can use the stovetop tip on the left.

6. Working with one tortilla at a time, crumble about 1 tablespoon queso fresco in a line across the center of the tortilla. Top with 1–2 tablespoons shredded beef mixture and roll tightly. Place seam-side down on a baking sheet sprayed with nonstick cooking spray. Spray tops of taquitos lightly with cooking spray and sprinkle with kosher salt.

7. Bake for 20–25 minutes or until the edges are golden brown. Remove from heat and allow to cool a few minutes before serving.

FREEZER INSTRUCTIONS:
Make as noted above through the step where you sprinkle the tops of the taquitos with salt. Place unbaked taquitos in a dish in a single layer, not touching each other, and set in the freezer. After frozen, place in zip-top bag, Foodsaver bag, or any other airtight container. To cook, place frozen taquitos on a baking sheet in a single layer and bake until edges are golden brown (about 30 minutes at 425 degrees F.).

Makes seasoning for 1–2 pounds of steak

⊙ **Quick and Easy**

SERVING SUGGESTIONS:
Serve as a salad (recipe below), with Guacamole (p. 50), Pico de Gallo (p. 48), and homemade Flour Tortillas (p. 37) for steak tacos or alongside quick and easy Black Beans (p. 202).

Chili-Lime Steak Salad

Serves 6–8

1 large head romaine lettuce

1 pint cherry or grape tomatoes, sliced in half

1 red onion, thinly sliced

1 (15-ounce) can black beans, drained and rinsed in cold water

1–2 avocados, sliced

1½ pounds Chili-Lime Steak

1 recipe Creamy Cilantro-Lime Ranch Dressing (p. 84)

Cilantro, for garnish

Crispy Corn Tortilla Strips (p. 141), optional

On individual plates, layer lettuce, tomatoes, onion, black beans, and avocados, and top with steak and dressing. Garnish with cilantro and tortilla strips if desired.

Chili-Lime Steak

Look no further than your spice rack for the ingredients in this Southwest-inspired steak rub! Add a little fresh-squeezed lime juice and your steaks will taste like something from a restaurant.

1–2 pounds boneless steak (flank steak works well)

Rub

1 teaspoon chili powder

1 teaspoon granulated garlic

½ teaspoon cumin

½ teaspoon coriander

½ teaspoon oregano

⅛–¼ teaspoon cayenne pepper*

¾ teaspoon kosher salt

¼ teaspoon freshly ground black pepper

1 lime, juiced (about 2 tablespoons lime juice)

1 tablespoon extra-virgin olive oil

*For a smoky rub, chipotle chili powder may be substituted for the cayenne pepper.

1. For the rub, combine spices in a small bowl. Add lime juice and olive oil and stir to combine.

2. Place the steak in a shallow dish (such as a 9 x 13-inch baking dish). Pour the spice mixture over the steak and then rub it in with your hands. Allow the steak to stand for 15 minutes. While the meat is standing, preheat your grill.

3. Place the steak on the grill over medium-high heat and cook for 5–7 minutes per side or until desired doneness is reached. Remove from grill and allow to stand for 5 minutes before slicing.

4. Slice steak against the grain into strips about ¼-inch thick.

Serves 4–6

🍲 **Slow Cooker**
☺ **Quick and Easy**

●●●●●●●●●●●●●●●

TIP: Using a cookie scoop is a great way to get meatballs that are all approximately the same size.

SLOW COOKER INSTRUCTIONS: After bringing the sauce mixture to a boil, transfer it to a slow cooker and add the meatballs. Cook on low for 3–4 hours.

FREEZER INSTRUCTIONS: Follow the directions as written through adding the meatballs to the sauce. Rather than placing the meatballs in the pan with the sauce, place them in a freezer-safe container and pour the sauce over them. Freeze for up to 3 months. When ready to cook, invert the container into a slow cooker and cook on low for 4–5 hours.

Sweet and Sour Meatballs

This is one of Kate's husband's all-time favorite meals. Serve these meatballs and the sweet, tangy sauce over hot rice with a side of stir-fried Asian vegetables.

1 pound extra-lean ground beef
2 tablespoons dehydrated onion
¼ teaspoon pepper
1 teaspoon kosher salt
1 egg, beaten
¼ cup bread crumbs

Sauce
¾ cup packed brown sugar
3 tablespoons flour
1½ cups water or pineapple juice
¼ cup white vinegar
3 tablespoons soy sauce

1. In a medium bowl, combine meatball ingredients. Shape into 1-inch balls and place on a baking sheet lined with aluminum foil and sprayed with nonstick cooking spray. Place under the broiler in your oven for 5–7 minutes or until the meatballs begin to brown.

2. In a large saucepan, whisk together the sauce ingredients and bring to a boil. Add the meatballs and reduce heat, cover, and simmer for 20 minutes, stirring often.

Cheesesteak Sandwiches

Sliced steak is sautéed in browning butter with sweet onions and bell peppers. Seasoned with coarse salt, freshly ground black pepper, and a little hot sauce, this recipe allows the flavors of each of the simple ingredients to shine. Topped with melted Provolone cheese, these fun sandwiches are both easy and crowd-pleasing.

Serves 4–6

⊕ **Quick and Easy**

●●●●●●●●●●●●●●●

TIP: The meat for these sandwiches needs to be very thinly sliced. If you have a food processor, you can freeze the steak for about 2 hours and then slice it in your food processor. If you don't, you can ask the butcher at the grocery store or the butcher shop to thinly slice 1 pound of steak or beef roast for you.

SERVING SUGGESTION: Serve with Oven-Baked Steak Fries (p. 182).

2 tablespoons butter

1 pound boneless steak (You can use any cut; since you're going to cut it up and season it heavily, there's no need to splurge on an expensive steak)

1 medium green bell pepper, thinly sliced

1 medium yellow onion, thinly sliced

Kosher salt

Freshly ground black pepper

Hot sauce, optional (such as Tabasco or Cholula)

Sliced Provolone cheese

4–6 Hoagie rolls

1. In a large skillet, melt butter over medium-high heat. When melted and bubbly, add steak. Stir constantly while it is cooking.

2. When the meat is about halfway cooked, add onions and green peppers. Season with salt, pepper, and hot sauce. Continue stirring until meat is cooked through and the onion and peppers are tender.

3. Spoon the meat filling into sliced rolls and add a slice of Provolone cheese. If desired, place the open-faced sandwiches onto a baking sheet and place the baking sheet under the broiler in your oven. Broil for 1–2 minutes or until bread is toasted and cheese is melted.

4. Serve immediately.

☆ **Make Ahead**

ROLLOVERS
Red bell pepper

● ● ● ● ● ● ● ● ● ● ● ● ● ● ● ●

SERVING SUGGESTION:
Serve with Baked Mushroom Rice
(p. 200).

FREEZER INSTRUCTIONS:
Prepare pies through the step of
brushing with the egg wash. Place the
baking sheet in the freezer and freeze
until the pies are solid. Transfer the
pies to a heavy-duty zip-top bag or
an airtight container and freeze until
ready to use. When ready, bake at 400
until the pies are golden brown, about
40–45 minutes.

Natchitoches Meat Pies

This recipe from Natchitoches (pronounced NACK-it-esh), Louisiana, simmers two types of ground meats in a flavorful broth. When the broth starts to evaporate and thicken, the mixture is spooned into a flaky pastry crust for a hand-held pie that's a Louisiana tradition and perfect for a holiday party.

½ pound lean ground beef

½ pound ground pork

½ green pepper, chopped

½ red pepper, chopped

1 onion, chopped

2 stalks celery, chopped

5–6 cloves garlic, minced

2 plus teaspoons Tony Chachere's Creole Seasoning or similar Cajun or Creole seasoning, to taste

Tabasco sauce to taste (start with about ¼ teaspoon)

1 (14.5-ounce) can low-sodium beef broth

Pie crust (p. 220), tripled

1 egg

¼ cup cold water

1. In a large skillet, brown ground beef and ground pork, breaking the meat into small pieces. When it's about halfway cooked, drain excess fat (if necessary) and then add green and red peppers, onion, celery, and garlic. Cook until vegetables are tender and onions are translucent.

2. Add 2 teaspoons Cajun seasoning and ¼ teaspoon Tabasco. Add beef broth and bring the mixture to a boil over high heat. Cook for about 20 minutes or until most of the liquid has evaporated. Season with additional Cajun seasoning and Tabasco if necessary, keeping in mind that the seasonings will mellow in the pie. You can refrigerate this mixture for 3–4 days before baking the pies.

3. Preheat oven to 400 degrees F. and spray a baking sheet with nonstick cooking spray.

4. Prepare pie crust and roll the entire ball onto a floured surface. For large (meal-sized) pies, use a bowl that's about 6 inches across the top; just invert the bowl onto the dough and trace a knife around it to cut the dough. For smaller, appetizer-sized pies, use a round cookie cutter.

5. Place about ¼ cup of the meat mixture onto one half of the dough circle

for meal-sized pies (about 1–2 teaspoons for appetizer pies), keeping about ½ inch to 1 inch from the edges. Fold the other side over and gently pinch the edges shut. For the decorative edge, crimp the edge with a fork or use your fingers to flute the edges. You could also use a calzone or empanada mold (used for these pictures).

6. Place prepared pies onto baking sheet. In a small bowl, whisk together egg and cold water and brush over the pies. Bake for 25–30 minutes or until golden brown.

ROLLOVER
Hamburger buns

●●●●●●●●●●●●●●●●●

TIP: When making burgers, you can use any ground beef you want, but the juiciest, most flavorful burgers tend to have a moderate amount of fat; when the meat is too fatty, the burgers are too heavy and greasy, and when the meat is too lean, the burgers tend to dry out and shrink quite a bit. The best burgers are made with meat that's between 80–90 percent lean, with 85 percent lean being a really great, happy medium.

SERVING SUGGESTIONS:
Serve with Sweet Potato Fries (p. 180), Oven-Baked Steak Fries (p. 182), or fresh fruit such as cubed watermelon (see p. 16).

Pineapple Bacon Burgers

Quick and easy, these crowd-pleasing burgers will be a huge hit at your next barbecue. To make things even simpler, use a high-quality bottled barbecue sauce (or buy some from your favorite barbecue restaurant) and cook the bacon ahead of time or buy pre-cooked bacon.

1 pound ground beef (see tip)

½ teaspoon kosher salt

¼ teaspoon freshly ground black pepper

High-quality barbecue sauce

4 slices pineapple

4 high-quality hamburger buns

8 slices bacon, cooked

1. Preheat grill to medium-high or about 400 degrees F.

2. Season ground beef with salt and black pepper. Gently combine with your hands, being careful not to overwork the meat.

3. Divide the meat into four portions and shape each portion into a patty.

4. Grill patties for 5–7 minutes per side or until desired doneness is reached. While burgers are cooking, brush each side with barbecue sauce once.

5. During the final minutes of cooking, lay pineapple slices and buns flat-side down onto the grill and heat them until they are heated through. The buns should be lightly toasted.

6. Remove burgers, pineapple slices, and buns from the grill. Place burgers on buns and then top each burger with a slice of pineapple and 2 slices of criss-crossed bacon. Drizzle with barbecue sauce and serve immediately.

⊕ **Quick and Easy**

ROLLOVERS
Italian sausage
Hamburger buns

●●●●●●●●●●●●●●●●

TIP: When working with ground meats, it's important to use your hands and be gentle because it can affect the texture of the final product.

SERVING SUGGESTIONS:
Serve with Oven-Baked Steak Fries (p. 182) or a salad topped with Italian Dressing (p. 86).

Italian Burgers

This quick and easy burger combines two types of meat plus a savory blend of seasonings for extra flavor and is smothered in melted fresh mozzarella and warm marinara sauce.

1 pound ground sirloin

8 ounces Italian turkey sausage

1½ teaspoons Italian seasoning

½ teaspoon kosher salt

¼ teaspoon black pepper

8–12 slices of fresh Mozzarella cheese

4–6 hamburger buns or Italian rolls

1 cup marinara sauce

Butter for toasting buns

1. Preheat grill or indoor grill pan.

2. Place ground beef in a mixing bowl. Remove casings from sausage if necessary and add to ground beef. Add Italian seasoning, salt, and pepper and use your hands to gently combine.

3. Divide beef mixture into equal portions, making either 6 small- to medium-sized burgers or 4 larger ones.

4. Place patties on grill. Cook for 3–4 minutes and then flip and cook an additional 3–4 minutes until cooked through, or until a thermometer registers 165 degrees F.

5. In the last minute of cooking, add a few slices of cheese to each burger. While cheese is melting, lightly butter buns and place face down on grill to toast, or place under the broiler until golden brown.

6. Spread about a tablespoon of marinara sauce on the bottom half of each bun. Place 1 patty on bottom half of each bun and top with an additional tablespoon of sauce. Add more if desired and top with other half of the bun.

Southwest Burgers

Using ground sirloin or chuck helps keep these burgers moist. Top them with smooth avocado, tangy Cotija cheese, and spicy, cool chipotle-lime mayonnaise.

Serves 4–6

⊙ **Quick and Easy**

ROLLOVERS
Fresh cilantro
Cotija or queso fresco cheese
Hamburger buns
Chipotle chilies with adobo

●●●●●●●●●●●●●●●

SERVING SUGGESTION:
Serve with Oven-Baked Steak Fries (p. 182) and fresh-cut watermelon (see p. 16).

½ cup mayonnaise (light mayonnaise works great)

6 teaspoons adobo sauce (from the canned chipotle chilies), divided

2 teaspoons lime juice

2 tablespoons chopped fresh cilantro

1½ pounds ground chuck or ground sirloin

1–1½ chipotle peppers canned in adobo sauce, seeds removed and minced (see Chipotle Beef Taquitos on p. 122 for tips on handling chipotles)

¼ cup grated onion

1 teaspoon garlic powder

½ teaspoon cumin

1½ teaspoons kosher salt

¼ teaspoon pepper

4–6 high-quality hamburger buns

1 tomato, sliced

1–2 avocados, sliced

Lettuce leaves, rinsed and patted dry

Pepper jack, Cotija, or queso fresco cheese, optional

1. Combine mayonnaise, 1½ teaspoons adobo sauce, lime juice, and cilantro in a small bowl. Cover and place in the refrigerator; this step can be done up to 2 days ahead of time.

2. Preheat grill or indoor grill pan.

3. Now place the beef in a bowl and gently crumble with your fingers. Add the peppers, 1½ tablespoons adobo sauce, onion, garlic powder, cumin, kosher salt, and pepper. Use your hands to gently mix the ingredients together.

4. Divide the ground beef mixture into 4–6 patties. Place the patties on the preheated grill and cook 5–7 minutes per side or until desired doneness is reached. While the burgers are cooking, lightly butter the buns and place them face-down on the grill for 1–2 minutes to toast them. If desired, during the last few minutes of cooking, you can add some queso fresco, Cotija, or Pepper jack cheese.

5. Remove burgers and buns from heat. Spread some of the lime-chipotle mayonnaise mixture over the buns and then assemble the burgers with the grilled patties, lettuce, sliced tomatoes, and sliced avocado.

Serves approximately 12–14

 **Slow Cooker**

●●●●●●●●●●●●●●●●

SERVING SUGGESTIONS:
Serve with Oven-Baked Steak Fries
(p. 182), Stuffed Blue Cheese Potatoes
(p. 183), or Baked Mushroom Rice
(p. 200).

FREEZER INSTRUCTIONS:
Place seared roast in a freezer-safe
container. Sprinkle with onion soup mix
and add the beef broth. When ready
to cook, turn the container into the
slow cooker and add 2 cups water. Add
about 1–2 hours onto the cooking time.

Slow Cooker French Dip Sandwiches

*This is hands-down one of the most popular recipes on our blog. A beef roast is
slowly simmered all day until it is full of flavor and fall-apart tender. Served hot
on top of a crusty roll with Swiss cheese and au jus on the side, this sandwich
is perfect for an easy weeknight dinner as well as a fun and festive holiday meal.*

2 tablespoons olive oil

1 (2½–3 pounds) beef roast

Kosher salt

Freshly ground black pepper

2 (1-ounce) packages dry onion soup mix

2 cups water

2 (14.5-ounce) cans beef broth

1 (16-ounce) package sliced Swiss
  cheese

Crusty buns or rolls (or Hoagies on p. 32)

1. Heat olive oil in a large pot or skillet over medium-high heat. While oil is
   heating, sprinkle all sides of the roast with kosher salt and freshly ground
   pepper.

2. When the oil is very hot, carefully place the roast in the pan and sear it
   on all sides. This shouldn't take more than a few minutes—you just want
   to quickly brown the roast to add flavor and seal in the juices.

3. Transfer the roast to your slow cooker. Sprinkle onion soup mix over the
   roast and add water and beef broth.

4. Cook on high for 4–6 hours or on low for 8–10 hours. You can also cook it
   on high until it begins to boil and then switch the heat setting to low; this
   is our preferred method because it seems to make the meat more tender,
   but it's not always possible to be there to switch the heat setting in the
   middle of the day.

5. When the meat shreds easily with a fork, shred the entire roast. Serve
   on sliced crusty rolls with a slice of Swiss cheese. If desired, you can
   slide these under the broiler on your oven to toast the bun and melt the
   cheese. Serve with the juices from the slow cooker as au jus for dipping.

ROLLOVER
Fresh ginger

●●●●●●●●●●●●●●●●

TIP: If you don't have a grill, you can also cook flank steak under the broiler. Place the steak on a broiler pan on the upper rack and broil for about 5–10 minutes per side, depending on the size of the steak. Because this particular marinade has sugar in it, you'll want to watch carefully so it doesn't burn. If you see the sugar burning too much, then you might want to move your rack down.

SERVING SUGGESTION:
Serve with Caramelized Green Beans (p. 188) and Sweet and Savory Coconut Rice (p. 203).

Pineapple-Ginger Flank Steak

Tangy pineapple juice combines with fresh ginger, salty soy sauce, and sweet brown sugar in this amazing flank steak marinade.

¾ cup pineapple juice

1 tablespoon minced fresh ginger

¼ cup soy sauce

6 tablespoons brown sugar

¼ cup canola oil

4–5 garlic cloves, minced

Up to 2 pounds flank steak

1. Whisk together first 6 ingredients for the marinade until combined. Remove ¼ cup of the marinade and set aside.

2. Score flank steak about ⅛-inch deep with a knife diagonally on both sides to tenderize the meat.

3. Place the steak in large zip-top bag and pour the marinade (excluding the ¼ cup of reserved marinade) over it. Refrigerate for 8 hours or overnight.

4. Remove from the fridge 30 minutes before grilling. Place the steak on a preheated grill and cook until the steak is still slightly pink on the inside or for 5–10 minutes per side, depending on the size of the steak.

5. Use the ¼ cup marinade you set aside to brush over the steak in the last few minutes of grilling.

6. Remove the steak from the grill and let stand for 5 minutes before slicing. To serve, cut flank steak against the grain into thin slices.

How to Work with Fresh Ginger

WHERE DO I FIND IT?

Ginger is an interesting-looking item. It can be found in most major grocery stores. It is usually found against the wall in the produce section, often by the Asian ingredients you can buy in bulk. Don't be afraid of the price; ginger is usually sold by the pound and the average recipe uses a very small amount.

HOW DO I PICK A GOOD ONE?

There will be all different shapes and sizes. You want to look for one that is firm, with light brown skin. Avoid any that are overly soft, have really dark or wet spots, or look dried out or shriveled. Feel free to break a knob off a larger piece, if necessary.

HOW DO I PEEL IT?

To cook with ginger, you'll want to peel off the skin. It's very thin and comes off easily with the right technique. The easiest way to do it is with a spoon. Hold the ginger in your non-dominant hand and run the tip of a spoon down the side and you'll see the skin peels right off, even around the knobs. You could also use a sharp paring knife and carefully remove the skin while preserving as much of the inner flesh as possible.

WHAT DO I DO WITH IT?

When you are left with a peeled piece, you can mince it up with a sharp knife into small pieces, or you can also use a cheese grater or a microplane if you need it to be fine. You will find the stringy texture easier to grate if it's frozen, so try putting it in the freezer for 15–20 minutes before using, if you plan to grate it.

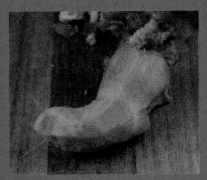

HOW DO I STORE THE EXTRA GINGER?

One of the best tips to know about ginger is that it freezes well, so when you're done and have leftovers, just pop the remaining ginger into a zip-top freezer bag and toss it in the freezer. When you are ready to use it again, just grate it frozen with a cheese grater.

WHAT SHOULD I USE IT FOR?

You'll see fresh ginger pop up in many of our Asian, Polynesian, and Thai dishes. It's often used in marinades, sauces, and salad dressings. It's also great finely minced and added to things such as fried rice and stir-fry dishes.

ROLLOVERS
Fresh ginger
Fresh cilantro

TIP: For instructions on cutting man-goes see p. 25.

Steak and Mango Salad

Garlic, ginger, soy sauce, and brown sugar are whisked together in the Polynesian-inspired steak marinade that also acts as the dressing for the salad. Slices of the grilled steak sit on top of leafy greens, sweet mangoes, crisp red onion slices, and creamy avocados and are topped with the sweet and savory dressing.

1 pound flank steak

½ cup caramelized macadamia nuts

½ teaspoon kosher salt

¼ teaspoon black pepper

1 head of romaine or red-leaf lettuce, rinsed, patted dry, and torn into bite-size pieces

1 red onion, thinly sliced

2 mangoes, sliced

1 large or 2 small avocados, sliced

½ cup roughly chopped cilantro

Dressing and Marinade

½ cup freshly squeezed orange juice

¼ cup plus 2 tablespoons fresh lime juice

¼ cup plus 2 tablespoons soy sauce

½ cup brown sugar

1½ tablespoons freshly grated ginger

4 cloves garlic, pressed or finely minced

¼ cup olive oil

½ cup canola oil

1. For the dressing and marinade, in a small mixing bowl, whisk together the orange juice, lime juice, soy sauce, brown sugar, ginger, and garlic until sugar is dissolved. Continue whisking while slowly drizzling in the oils until combined. Reserve about ¾ cup of the dressing and place the rest of the mixture in a large zip-top bag.

2. Lightly score the flank steak in a diagonal pattern on both sides. Place steak in the zip-top bag with the marinade and allow to marinate in the fridge for at least 8 hours, preferably overnight.

3. Caramelize the macadamia nuts according to the directions on p. 254.

4. Remove the steak from the refrigerator about 30 minutes prior to cooking and allow to come to room temperature. You'll want to let the dressing portion sit at room temperature during this time as well.

5. Heat an outdoor grill to medium-high heat. If an outdoor grill is not available, use the broiler in your oven or an indoor grill pan. Remove the steak from the bag and let any excess marinade drip off. Sprinkle steak

lightly with salt and pepper. Cook for about 5–8 minutes on each side or until done. In order to stay tender, flank steak should still be pink in the middle, but nicely seared on the outside. When done, remove from grill and wait at least 5 minutes before cutting to let the juices redistribute. Then slice into thin slices.

6. To assemble the salads, divide the lettuce onto plates and top with slices of mango, avocado, and red onion. Add steak slices and drizzle with dressing. Sprinkle macadamia nuts and cilantro on top.

TIP: It's important to sear fatty roasts like pork shoulder because it prevents the final result from being overly greasy.

SERVING SUGGESTIONS:
Make fresh Mexican restaurant-style salads with homemade Flour Tortillas (p. 37), chopped romaine lettuce, rinsed and drained black beans, Cilantro-Lime Vinaigrette (p. 88), or Creamy Cilantro-Lime Ranch Dressing (p. 85), Lime-Cilantro Rice with Pineapple (p. 204), Pico de Gallo (p. 48), crumbled Cotija cheese, Guacamole (p. 50), and Crispy Corn Tortilla Strips (see facing page).

Mexican-Style Sweet Shredded Pork

This sweet pork is similar to the pork found in popular fresh Mexican restaurants. If you don't want to make salads, try wrapping it in fresh flour tortillas, placing in a 9 x 13-inch baking dish, and making the green enchilada sauce for Chili Verde on p. 146; pour over the burritos, sprinkle with Monterey Jack cheese, and bake at 350 degrees F. until the cheese is melted and bubbly.

4 pounds boneless pork shoulder roast

½ teaspoon kosher salt

¼ teaspoon black pepper

2 teaspoons chili powder

1 teaspoon onion powder

1–2 tablespoons vegetable oil

2 (10-ounce) cans enchilada sauce

1 cup brown sugar, divided

½ cup salsa

½ tablespoon Worcestershire sauce

¼ cup apple juice

1. Trim the visible fat from the roast and sprinkle with salt, pepper, chili powder, and onion powder. Use your hands to massage the spices over all sides of the meat.

2. Heat the oil in a large skillet over medium-high heat. Sear the pork roast for about 1 minute on all sides or until meat surface is golden brown.

3. While the meat is searing, combine the enchilada sauce, ⅔ cup brown sugar, salsa, Worcestershire sauce, and apple juice in a slow-cooker. Add the pork, cover, and cook on low for 7 hours with lid on the entire time.

4. Remove pork and shred, discarding any pieces of fat. Add the additional ⅓ cup brown sugar to slow cooker and turn heat to high. Add shredded meat. Simmer with lid off for 30 minutes.

Crispy Corn Tortilla Strips

Canola oil, enough to fill a large skillet ½–1-inch deep

Kosher salt, to taste

Up to 12 corn tortillas

1. Heat about ½–1 inch oil in a large skillet.

2. While the oil is heating, use a pizza wheel to cut the tortillas into thin (about ¼-inch wide) strips.

3. Test the oil's temperature by tossing a small corner of corn tortilla into the oil; if it sinks, continue heating. If it sizzles violently, turn the heat down. If the strip sinks and then quickly rises to the top and bubbles, the oil is ready.

4. Cook all the tortilla strips (in batches, if necessary), and drain on a paper towel. Sprinkle with kosher salt and serve as desired.

⊙ **Quick and Easy**

ROLLOVERS
Fresh parsley
Fresh cilantro
Fresh oregano

●●●●●●●●●●●●●●●●

TIP: If you can't get any fresh oregano, use the fresh parsley and cilantro
and then substitute 1 tablespoon + 1
teaspoon dry oregano.

SERVING SUGGESTION:
Serve with Quick and Easy Black Beans
(p. 202) and Lime-Cilantro Rice with
Pineapple (p. 204).

Grilled Pork Tenderloin with Chimichurri

*Fresh herbs and garlic quickly infuse delicate pork tenderloin with delectable,
savory flavor. The chimichurri sauce is equally delicious with any cut of steak.
When cooked on the grill, no one will be able to resist it!*

2–3 pounds pork tenderloin (2
small-medium pork tenderloins)

Chimichurri Sauce
1½ cups chopped parsley
1½ cups chopped cilantro
½ cup loosely packed oregano leaves*
2 tablespoons fresh lime juice

1 tablespoon red wine vinegar
3 tablespoons chopped garlic (6–7
cloves)
1 teaspoon kosher salt
¼ teaspoon freshly ground black pepper
¼ teaspoon red pepper flakes
½ cup extra-virgin olive oil

1. Place pork tenderloins in a large zip-top bag and set aside.

2. To make the chimichurri, place parsley, cilantro, oregano, lime juice,
   vinegar, garlic, salt, and pepper in a food processor. Pulse several times
   until finely chopped. Transfer mixture to a bowl. Add red pepper flakes
   and then stir in olive oil by hand.

3. Remove ½–¾ cup chimichurri and pour it over the pork tenderloins. You
   just need enough to coat them well. Seal bag and set aside to marinate
   for about an hour or longer if you need to. Cover the reserved chimichurri
   and set aside.

4. When ready to cook, preheat the grill. Remove the tenderloins from
   the bag and let excess marinade drip off. Place on the grill and cook for
   about 5–8 minutes before flipping to the other side. You want the internal
   temperature to be about 160 degrees F., so check with a thermometer
   and take it off the grill when it reaches 155–158 degrees F. since it will
   continue to cook a bit as it sits. Remove from the grill and let it stand
   5 minutes before cutting. Slice, and serve with remaining chimichurri
   drizzled on top.

🍲 **Slow Cooker**

●●●●●●●●●●●●●●●●

TIP: To help keep the ribs intact, don't remove the silvery membrane.

SERVING SUGGESTION:
Serve with Grilled Corn on the Cob (p. 196), Grilled Potatoes and Onions (p. 184), and watermelon (see the tutorial on p. 16).

Baby Back Ribs

Baby back pork ribs simmer all day in a braising liquid that's almost good enough to drink by itself, yielding fall-off-the-bone tenderness. They're then finished off on the grill with a brushing of your favorite barbecue sauce. Trust us, you'll compare all other ribs you'll ever eat to these.

3 cups pineapple juice

1½ cups brown sugar

1½ teaspoons mustard powder

⅓ cup ketchup

⅓ cup red wine vinegar

1½ tablespoons lemon juice

2 tablespoons soy sauce

½ teaspoon ground cloves

2 teaspoons ground ginger

4 cloves garlic, minced

½ teaspoon cayenne pepper

2–3 pounds baby back pork ribs

1 bottle high-quality barbecue sauce (we use Stubbs)

1. In a large slow cooker, whisk together all the ingredients except the ribs and barbecue sauce.

2. Cut the ribs into 3–4-inch pieces; place into the slow cooker. Cook on low for 6–8 hours or until the ribs are very tender but not completely falling off the bone. Remove from the liquid.

3. Preheat outdoor grill to medium. Baste ribs with barbecue sauce and grill for 3–4 minutes per side or until they are glazed and the sauce is beginning to char.

Glazed Pork Chops with Apricot-Ginger Sauce

Pork is so mild and sweet that it pairs naturally with the flavors of apricot and pineapple in this recipe.

●●●●●●●●●●●●●●●

SERVING SUGGESTION:
Serve with green vegetables like Oven-Roasted Broccoli (without the Parmesan cheese, p. 199), or steamed carrots.

¾ teaspoon kosher salt

½ teaspoon garlic powder

½ teaspoon onion powder

¼ teaspoon freshly ground black pepper

4 boneless loin pork chops, about ½-inch thick each

2 teaspoons olive oil

1 tablespoon butter

1 clove garlic, minced

2 teaspoons minced ginger (or bottled minced ginger)

½ cup chicken broth

⅔ cup bottled apricot-pineapple preserves

1. Heat a large skillet over medium-high heat.

2. While the pan is heating, combine the salt, garlic and onion powders, and pepper. Sprinkle half of spice mixture evenly over one side of pork chops.

3. When the pan is hot, add the olive oil. Place pork, spice side down, in the hot pan. Sprinkle the remaining spice mixture on the top of the pork chops. Cook the pork for 3 minutes and then flip and cook 3 additional minutes. Remove the pork from the pan and cover with foil to keep warm.

4. Reduce the heat to medium and add the butter. When melted, add the garlic and ginger. Sauté for about 30 seconds while stirring. Add the chicken broth and bring to a simmer. Use a spatula to scrape up the browned bits from the bottom of the pan and continue to simmer for 1 minute.

5. Whisk in the preserves. Bring the sauce to a simmer and return the pork to the pan. Cook for an additional 2–3 minutes on each side or until cooked through to an internal temperature of 160 degrees F.

6. Remove from heat and let the pork chops rest for 5 minutes before serving. Serve over white or brown rice and spoon the sauce from the pan over each piece of pork.

ROLLOVER
Fresh cilantro

●●●●●●●●●●●●●●●

TIP: Pork sirloin roasts are extremely lean and tender and a great alternative to boneless, skinless chicken breasts.

VARIATION: To make green enchilada sauce, omit the pork.

SLOW COOKER INSTRUCTIONS: Combine sautéed pork, onions, garlic, tomatillo mixture, and chicken broth in a slow cooker and cook on low all day until desired consistency is reached.

FREEZER INSTRUCTIONS: Follow recipe through step 2. Place all ingredients in a freezer-safe container and freeze for up to 3 months. When ready to cook, invert the container into the slow cooker and cook on low for 9–10 hours. Serve as directed.

SERVING SUGGESTION: Serve with soft Flour Tortillas (p. 37), Guacamole (p. 50), and Pico de Gallo (p. 48).

Pork Tacos with Chili Verde

Chicken broth and tangy tomatillos are the base for this traditional Mexican pork dish. Slow-simmered with garlic, onions, hot peppers, and seasonings, this is comfort food at its best.

2–3 tablespoons extra-virgin olive oil

2 pounds pork sirloin roast, rinsed, trimmed of fat, and cut into ½-inch cubes

2½ teaspoons kosher salt, divided

½ teaspoon black pepper, divided

1 large onion, minced

5–6 cloves garlic, minced or pressed

1½ pounds tomatillos, husked and quartered or halved

2 green peppers, chopped

1–2 jalapeños, seeded and membranes removed, if desired

½ bunch cilantro, coarsely chopped

4 cups chicken broth

1½ teaspoons cumin

2–3 tablespoons sugar

1. In a large saucepan or stockpot, heat olive oil over medium heat. Add the pork cubes and season with 1 teaspoon salt and ¼ teaspoon pepper. Add onion and garlic. Cook, stirring frequently, until everything is tender and fragrant.

2. While onions are sautéing, combine tomatillos, green peppers, jalapeños, and cilantro in your blender. Process until smooth; you may have to do it in batches and/or add some chicken broth to make the sauce easy to blend.

3. Pour the tomatillo mixture over the pork and add chicken broth, salt, pepper, cumin, and sugar. Simmer for 30 minutes to 1 hour, depending on the consistency you want. You can also turn the heat to high and boil the chile verde uncovered until the desired consistency is reached, just be sure to stir frequently to avoid scorching.

⊙ **Quick and Easy**

●●●●●●●●●●●●●●●●●

TIP: Because pork tenderloin is so lean, be careful not to overcook it. Instant-read meat thermometers are inexpensive and will tell you when the internal temperature reaches 160–165 degrees F. When cooked correctly (and allowed to rest for 5–10 minutes after cooking), the roast should be very juicy but not pink.

Roasted Pork Tenderloin

Pork tenderloin is extremely lean and tender. Marinate it ahead of time and then roast it up in no time and you have a super-easy main dish that's sure to impress!

1–1½ pounds pork tenderloin

1. Choose from one of the following flavor combinations. After following the specific marinade instructions, preheat oven to 400 degrees F. Remove the pork from the bag and place the tenderloin on a foil-lined baking dish. Place in the preheated oven and bake until internal temperature of the roast reaches 160 degrees F., about 20–25 minutes.

2. Let stand for 5 minutes and then slice into ½-inch pieces. Spoon pan juices over roast before serving.

Rosemary-Balsamic Pork Tenderloin

4–5 cloves garlic, finely minced

1 teaspoon crushed rosemary

1 teaspoon kosher salt

¼ teaspoon black pepper

1½ teaspoons balsamic vinegar

2 teaspoons olive oil

1. Combine garlic, rosemary, salt, and pepper. Massage the seasonings all over the pork loin.

2. Whisk together the balsamic vinegar and olive oil.

3. Place the seasoned pork tenderloin in a zip-top bag and add the oil and vinegar combination. Seal the bag and refrigerate for 4–10 hours. Cook according to the instructions.

Ginger-Soy Pork Tenderloin

3 tablespoons soy sauce

1 tablespoon olive oil

2 tablespoons brown sugar

2 cloves garlic, minced

½ teaspoon ground ginger or ½ tablespoon fresh minced ginger

1 teaspoon fresh lemon juice

1. In a small bowl, whisk together the soy sauce, olive oil, brown sugar, garlic, ginger, and lemon juice.

2. Place the tenderloin in a large zip-top bag and pour the marinade over the pork. Allow to marinate 4–10 hours. Cook according to the directions.

Sweet and Sour Marinade (Pictured)

½ cup ketchup

½ cup apple jelly

1½ teaspoons apple cider vinegar

¾ teaspoon chili powder

1 teaspoon garlic powder

½ teaspoon onion powder

½ teaspoon kosher salt

⅛ teaspoon black pepper

1. In a small bowl, combine all the marinade ingredients. Reserve ¼ cup of this marinade and pour the rest over the pork tenderloin in a zip-top bag. Marinate 4–10 hours.

2. Cook according to the directions, basting with the reserved marinade during the last 10 minutes of cooking.

Indian-Spiced Pork Skewers

Serves 6–8

Tender pieces of lean pork marinate in traditional Indian spices before they're skewered with chunks of red bell pepper and onion and grilled.

●●●●●●●●●●●●●●●●
SERVING SUGGESTION:
Serve with Sweet and Savory Coconut Rice (p. 203).

1½–2 pounds pork tenderloin or sirloin pork roast

2 red bell peppers

1 large onion

1 tablespoon pressed or minced garlic

1½ teaspoons kosher salt

½ tablespoon cumin

1 tablespoon curry powder

½ tablespoon coriander

⅛ teaspoon cayenne pepper

¼ cup fresh lemon juice

3 tablespoons extra-virgin olive oil

1 tablespoon water

1. Cut the pork into 1½-inch chunks and place in a zip-top bag. Set aside.

2. Prepare the peppers and onion by chopping them into squares. Refrigerate, covered, until ready to use.

3. Mix the garlic and salt in a small bowl with the cumin, curry, coriander, and cayenne pepper. Add the fresh lemon juice (not bottled!) and olive oil and combine well.

4. Pour the spice mixture into the zip-top bag with the pork. Seal the bag and then gently mash the bag to combine the seasonings with the pork. Refrigerate for at least 3–4 hours.

5. Before skewering, make sure to soak bamboo skewers for at least 30 minutes in water. Preheat an outdoor grill to medium heat.

6. Alternately thread the pork chunks with the red pepper and onion. Grill on the preheated grill for about 10 minutes, turning the skewers often to avoid burning. If you've cut your pork chunks an inch or smaller, they will be done very quickly, so be careful not to overcook. Serve immediately.

Jambalaya

This Creole classic starts with the revered trio of Louisiana cooking (green peppers, onions, and celery) and is combined with garlic, smoky ham and sausage, rice, tomato sauce, and Creole seasoning in a dish that you could use to clean out your fridge and serve to guests at the same time!

Serves 6–8

ROLLOVERS
Green onions
Smoked sausage

●●●●●●●●●●●●●●●

TIP: Andouille sausage is delicious, but it can be quite spicy; you can control the heat by finding a flavorful smoked sausage from Texas or Louisiana and then adding Cajun or Creole seasoning for a little heat.

2½ cups long-grain white rice

4¾ cups plus 1 tablespoon water

1–2 tablespoons white vinegar

6–8 ounces of high-quality smoked sausage (try and buy local smoked sausage from a butcher or high-end grocer. See the tip on buying sausage)

6–8 ounces ham (you can also substitute leftover Fauxtisserie Chicken (p. 110), or cooked shrimp, crawfish, or lobster; however, you'll also need to compensate for the smoky flavor and the salt from the ham, so be prepared with liquid smoke and salt to taste)

2–3 tablespoons butter

1 medium onion, chopped

1 bunch green onions, chopped

1 green pepper, chopped

2 stalks celery, chopped

5–6 cloves of garlic, minced

1 (8-ounce) can tomato sauce

Cajun or Creole seasoning (we use Tony Chachere's Creole Seasoning)

1. Combine rice, water, and vinegar in a medium-large saucepan and cover with lid. Bring to a boil and then reduce heat to low and cook 20 minutes or until rice is cooked well. Remove from heat and allow to stand covered for an additional 5 minutes.

2. While rice is cooking, finely chop sausage and ham (a food processor makes this step easy) and set aside.

3. Melt butter over medium heat in a very large skillet. When the butter is hot and bubbly, add onion, green onions, green pepper, celery, and garlic and cook until tender. Add chopped meat and cook, stirring frequently, for about 10 minutes. Add tomato sauce and then add cooked rice. Stir to combine.

4. Season to taste with the Cajun seasoning. It's hot, so if you find that it's getting spicy enough for your taste but it's still not salty enough, leave the Cajun seasoning alone and just finish seasoning it with kosher salt. Cook for about 10 more minutes, stirring frequently. This recipe tastes even better the next day.

Pizza and Pasta

Facing page: Spinach and Feta Pasta, see page 172

How to Make Great Pizza in the Oven

If homemade pizza is fun in theory and ends hours later with mediocre pizza and a doughy crust, try following these steps for perfect pizza made in your oven! When you get comfortable making it in the oven, be sure to try making it on the grill (p. 156)!

1. Begin preparing your dough (p. 30). Complete steps through the first rise.

2. While dough is rising, prepare your desired sauce.

3. Preheat your oven (and your pizza stone, if you want) to 425 degrees F. While oven is heating, punch down dough and shape into a disc. Spray your work surface, rolling pin, and pizza stone with nonstick cooking spray. Place dough disc onto work surface. Roll and shape into a circle. (Disregard all of this, by the way, if you're a stinking dough-thrower). Very gently transfer the dough onto your pizza stone and continue to shape up to the edges of the stone.

4. Using a fork, prick several holes in the crust. Drizzle crust with a little olive oil and brush all the way up to the edges. Sprinkle with garlic salt. Both oiling and garlic salting the crust help crisp it up, give it a great flavor, and keep it from getting soggy in the middle.

5. Bake crust in preheated oven for 10–12 minutes or until golden. Remove from oven.

6. Spread a layer of sauce (if desired) over the surface of the crust. Top with whatever toppings you like. Sprinkle with oregano.

7. Return the pizza to the oven and bake 10–12 more minutes or until cheese is melted and the crust is golden brown. Allow the pizza to cool for about 5 minutes before slicing and serving to allow the cheese to set up a bit.

PIZZA STONE. This is essential for getting a deep, even heat and creating a great texture for your pizza crust.

FRENCH ROLLING PIN. A regular rolling pin will work in a pinch, but French rolling pins have tapered edges that make it easier to roll out large quantities of flat dough.

DOUGH. We love the breadstick dough on p. 30.

SAUCE. Try Pizza Sauce (p. 155), Guiltless Alfredo Sauce (p. 158), Fresh Basil Pesto (p. 47), or add some roasted garlic (p. 52) to softened butter.

OLIVE OIL. It makes your crust crispy and delicious.

GARLIC SALT. This helps make your crust flavorful and crispy. Garlic Bread Seasoning (p. 53) works great, too.

CHEESE. About 8 ounces of shredded or deli-sliced cheese is perfect for an average pizza. Mozzarella is a great, versatile choice.

DRIED OREGANO. This is the "secret ingredient."

DESIRED TOPPINGS. Whatever you like on pizza!

Pizza Sauce

You'll never go back to using bottled marinara sauce on pizza after you try this. It comes together in a matter of minutes and tastes like something a professional would make!

1 (6-ounce) can tomato paste

6 ounces water (just use the empty tomato paste can)

3 tablespoons Garlic Bread Seasoning (p. 53)

1 tablespoon sugar or honey

¾ teaspoon onion powder

¼ teaspoon red pepper flakes, optional

Empty tomato paste into a bowl and add water a few tablespoons at a time, stirring constantly until combined. Add remaining ingredients, stir to combine, and allow to stand until ready to use. Covers two average-sized pizzas.

Makes about 1½ cups

☆ **Make Ahead**

☉ **Quick and Easy**

🌿 **Vegetarian**

●●●●●●●●●●●●●●●●

SERVING SUGGESTION:
Serve on pizza or as a dipping sauce for Stuffed Pizza Rolls (p. 164) or Breadsticks (p. 30).

FREEZER INSTRUCTIONS:
This sauce freezes extremely well; just place any unused sauce in a zip-top bag or a small freezer-safe container and freeze for up to 3 months.

How to Make Great Pizza on the Grill

Once you're comfortable making pizza in the oven, you've got to try making it on the grill! The smoky flavor and thin crust tastes like something from a top-notch pizza joint, not your backyard!

DOUGH. You can use any pizza dough—whatever you normally use to make pizza at home. We love the dough for Breadsticks (p. 30), which makes about 2 larger pizzas or 4–6 smaller, individual pizzas. You can also buy dough—many grocery stores and bakeries sell fresh, raw pizza dough.

TOPPINGS. We suggest going a little lighter than normal on the toppings for a few reasons. First, it will keep the pizzas easy to work with and easy to move around. Secondly, the crust will cook quickly, so you want to make sure all your toppings are cooked through. Finally, the grill adds so much flavor and texture that you don't want (or need) to overpower it. Grilled pizza works great sauceless, or try it with our Pizza Sauce (p. 155), barbecue sauce, or Guiltless Alfredo Sauce (p. 158).

OLIVE OIL. You'll want to brush both the pizza and the grill with it.

LARGE SPATULA. You'll need to flip the dough on the grill, so the spatula needs to be big. If you've ever wondered what to do with the pizza paddle you got for your wedding, today's your day.

OTHER UTENSILS. For spreading the sauces and distributing the ingredients.

1. Preheat your grill. This is an important step. The rack needs to be nice and hot so the dough will start cooking immediately. Also, the overall temperature needs to be hot in order to act like an oven when the lid is closed. Set your gas grill to medium heat and leave the lid shut.

2. Next, get all of your toppings ready. You have to move very quickly while at the grill, so everything needs to be prepared and easy to grab. To make things easy, set up a platter with everything you need and keep it next to the grill.

3. When your dough is ready, roll it out with a rolling pin, or even just use your hands to press and stretch it. Now throw all your preconceived pizza notions out the window. You don't need to make round pizza. They can be rectangular or irregular, which is part of the beauty of grilled pizza.

4. It is easiest to make several small pizzas, especially if you're trying this for the first time. We like to do 4 small pizzas. A 6- to 8-inch pizza will easily feed one very hungry adult or a couple of hungry kids. Another benefit of doing several smaller pizzas is that you can try out a bunch of different topping combos. Kids love having their own! If you want to go big, this dough will make two 9- to 10-inch pizzas.

5. Once your dough is flattened out, drizzle a little olive oil on one side and brush it around.

6. Toss the dough, oiled-side down, straight onto the grill and then shut the lid immediately. Turn the heat to medium-low. How long you cook it all depends on the heat of the grill and the thickness of the dough, but it usually only takes about 5 minutes or less. Have a spatula handy to lift up the dough and check it. You'll want to see nice brown grill marks, but avoid burning it. If you can tell that your dough is cooking too fast and too hot, you may want to use indirect heat. For a gas grill with multiple burners, turn off the burner directly under the pizza, but leave the others on. For a charcoal grill, move the charcoal to one side of the grill and place the pizza on the other side. Right before you flip it, brush a little olive oil on the uncooked side.

7. As soon as you flip it, grab that tray with your toppings and put them on the cooked side right away. Shut the lid again and leave it shut. The second side cooks pretty fast. If the bottom of your pizza is done, but the top still needs to cook, you can place it on an upper rack if you have one.

8. Take a peek at the bottom crust and as soon as it's done and your cheese is melted, grab a spatula and pull it off. Serve immediately.

⊙ **Quick and Easy**
🌱 **Vegetarian**

ROLLOVER
Cream cheese

●●●●●●●●●●●●●●●●

TIP: For the Parmesan cheese in this recipe, use a wedge of ungrated Parmesan and grate it yourself with a microplane or even in your food processor. Pregrated Parmesan cheese is too dry and while your sauce will still taste great, it will be lumpy.

SERVING SUGGESTION:
This sauce is super versatile. Drizzle it over steamed vegetables, use it as a dip for Breadsticks (p. 30) or as a sauce or dip for Pizza (p. 154 and 156).

FREEZER INSTRUCTIONS:
After step three, transfer the mixture to an 8 x 8-inch disposable aluminum baking pan. Sprinkle with cheese and cover tightly with aluminum foil. Freeze for up to 3 months. When ready to cook, preheat the oven to 400 degrees F. and bake, covered, for 90 minutes or until the casserole is cooked through and the cheese is melted and bubbly.

Guiltless Alfredo Sauce

This is probably Kate's favorite of all of Sara's recipes. This sauce is garlicky and flavorful and doesn't leave you feeling weighed down. Try serving it on top of noodles with grilled chicken and a side of broccoli.

2 cups low-fat milk

⅓ cup (3 ounces) low-fat cream cheese

2 tablespoons flour

1 teaspoon kosher salt

1 tablespoon butter

3 garlic cloves, minced

1 cup freshly grated Parmesan cheese (see tip)

1. In a blender, blend the milk, cream cheese, flour, and salt until smooth and set aside.

2. In a large, nonstick saucepan, melt butter on medium-high heat and add the garlic. Sauté the garlic for about 30 seconds, stirring constantly to prevent the garlic from sticking and burning.

3. Add the milk mixture to the pan. Stir constantly for 3–4 minutes or until it just comes to a simmer. Keep stirring and let it cook for a few minutes more or until the sauce thickens, about 6–7 minutes.

4. Once the sauce has started to thicken, remove from heat. Whisk the cheese into the sauce and immediately cover the pan.

5. Allow the sauce to stand for at least 10 minutes before using. It will continue to thicken upon standing.

6. Serve immediately. Refrigerate leftovers for up to 5 days. The sauce will become very thick once refrigerated. To use it, reheat the sauce and add a little milk until the desired consistency is reached.

Pumpkin Alfredo

1 (8-ounce) package fresh pasta (cheese ravioli are wonderful!)

½ batch Guiltless Alfredo Sauce

½ tablespoon real butter

¼ cup finely minced onion

2 tablespoons chicken broth

1 tablespoon freshly chopped sage (or 1 teaspoon dry sage leaves)

½ tablespoon fresh thyme (or ½ teaspoon dried thyme)

½ cup canned pumpkin

1. Cook the pasta according to package directions.

2. In a separate saucepan, melt the butter on medium heat. When melted, add onion and sauté until it is translucent and fragrant.

3. Add chicken broth and herbs. Use a spatula to deglaze the pan a bit and get any cooked bits of onion off the bottom. Add pumpkin and whisk to combine. Add alfredo sauce, stir to combine, and cook until heated through. Serve immediately over the cooked pasta.

Bacon Artichoke with Penne Bake

8 ounces penne or bowtie pasta

1 recipe Guiltless Alfredo Sauce

2 chicken breasts, grilled and chopped (about 2 cups chopped chicken)

6 ounces (½ package) cooked bacon, chopped

1 (14-ounce) jar marinated artichoke hearts, drained and chopped

½ cup chopped green onions (about 1 decent-sized bunch)

1 cup shredded mozzarella cheese, divided

Salt and pepper, to taste

1. Preheat oven to 350 degrees F.

2. Prepare pasta according to package directions.

3. While the pasta is cooking, prepare Guiltless Alfredo Sauce. When pasta is done, drain and add to the sauce. Toss with chopped chicken, bacon, artichoke hearts, green onions, and ½ cup mozzarella. Season to taste.

4. Transfer mixture to an 8 x 8-inch baking dish and sprinkle with remaining ½ cup mozzarella cheese. Cover with aluminum foil and bake for 20 minutes or until heated through and cheese is bubbly.

ROLLOVER

Spinach

●●●●●●●●●●●●●●●●

SERVING SUGGESTION:

Serve with a tossed green salad.

Spinach-Chicken Stromboli

Use either refrigerated pizza crust or homemade pizza dough for this calzone-like Italian meal.

1 refrigerated pizza crust or 1 recipe of Breadstick dough (p. 30)

2 teaspoons olive oil, divided

1½ teaspoons Italian Seasoning

3½ tablespoons canned Parmesan cheese, divided

1½ cups shredded mozzarella cheese

2 cups loosely packed spinach leaves

8 ounces shredded, cooked chicken breast (about 2 cups)

2 Roma tomatoes, diced

Favorite pasta sauces for dipping

1. Preheat oven to the temperature indicated on the dough package or recipe.

2. Working on a floured surface, roll pizza dough into a 12 x 15-inch rectangle. Brush 1½ teaspoons olive oil over entire surface of crust. Evenly sprinkle Italian seasoning and 2 tablespoons Parmesan on top.

3. Keeping remaining toppings one inch away from all edges, evenly spread the spinach leaves, shredded chicken, and tomatoes over the dough.

4. Working from the long end of the rectangle, roll up from one end to the other (like a cinnamon roll). Pinch seam shut and then pinch each end shut and tuck under toward seam.

5. Place seam-side down on a baking sheet sprayed lightly with nonstick spray. Brush remaining ½ teaspoon olive oil on top and sprinkle with remaining 1½ tablespoons Parmesan cheese. Gently cut 3 slits along the top of the Stromboli.

6. Bake in preheated oven for 15–20 minutes or until the top is golden brown. Cool for 10–15 minutes before slicing into 1-inch slices. Serve with marinara and/or Alfredo sauce for dipping.

Spaghetti and Meatballs

Flavorful meatballs simmer in a divine sauce made with crushed tomatoes and Italian herbs. Don't forget to check out the freezer instructions for an easy meal on a cold, winter night.

●●●●●●●●●●●●●●●●

SERVING SUGGESTION:
Serve with a green salad and fresh, crusty bread.

FREEZER INSTRUCTIONS:
Prepare meatballs as directed, but divide the meatballs between 2 freezer-safe containers. Prepare sauce through adding all ingredients to the pan, but don't simmer; rather, divide the sauce between the 2 containers. Freeze until ready to use. When ready to use, place in slow cooker and cook on low for about 5–6 hours, although you'll want to keep an eye on the sauce and make sure it's not burning if you go for the whole 6 hours.

1–2 tablespoons olive oil

1 large onion, chopped

4–5 cloves garlic, minced or pressed

2 (28-ounce) cans crushed tomatoes

1 (16-ounce) can tomato sauce

1–2 tablespoons sugar (to taste)

2 teaspoons basil

1 teaspoon Italian seasoning

Pinch of red pepper flakes

Salt and pepper to taste

Pinch of baking soda (to help neutralize the acid)

1 recipe Italian Meatballs (p. 163)

1 (16-ounce) package dry pasta, cooked per instructions

Freshly shredded Parmesan cheese, to taste

1. Heat olive oil in a large skillet. Add onion and garlic and cook until onions are translucent and garlic is fragrant. Add remaining sauce ingredients and combine well. Bring to a simmer and add meatballs. Simmer on low, uncovered, until desired consistency is reached—about 25–30 minutes for a sauce that's of medium consistency.

2. Serve over hot pasta with Parmesan cheese.

Italian Meatballs

These incredibly flavorful meatballs can be used in our Italian Meatball Soup (p. 105) or for Spaghetti and Meatballs (p. 162) or topped with marinara sauce and melted provolone in a classic meatball sub.

½ pound ground beef

½ pound sweet Italian sausage

2 eggs, beaten

¼ cup plain bread crumbs

2 tablespoons freshly grated Parmesan cheese

1 teaspoon basil

½ teaspoon parsley

¼ cup dehydrated onion

1 clove garlic, minced

1 teaspoon kosher salt

½ teaspoon pepper

1. Turn on the oven broiler. Line a baking sheet with aluminum foil and spray with nonstick cooking spray. Set aside.

2. Gently combine all ingredients in a medium bowl. Shape the meat mixture into meatballs. A cookie scoop is great for helping maintain a uniform size, although you can make them bigger or smaller if you'd like. Place the meatballs on the prepared baking sheet.

3. Place the baking sheet in the oven and cook for 7–10 minutes or until the meatballs are becoming brown and fragrant. If you're going to be simmering the meatballs in soup or some type of sauce, it's best to cook them until they're just brown so they can finish cooking in the sauce or soup and release some of their flavor into the cooking liquid.

Makes about 36 meatballs, using a standard cookie scoop

ROLLOVER

Italian sausage

FREEZER INSTRUCTIONS:

Broil the meatballs until just brown and they can hold their shape; they won't be cooked through. Remove the baking sheet from the oven and allow to cool, then place the entire baking sheet in the freezer and freeze until the meatballs are solid. Transfer the meatballs to a freezer-safe container and freeze for up to 3 months. If you're making Spaghetti and Meatballs (p. 162) or Italian Meatball Soup (p. 105), drop the frozen meatballs into the simmering sauce and continue simmering until the meatballs are completely cooked.

●●●●●●●●●●●●●●●●●

VARIATION: In place of pizza toppings, use cubed cheddar, shredded chicken, and cooked bacon. Combine 1 teaspoon packaged dry ranch dressing with 1½ tablespoons powdered Parmesan cheese and set aside. After assembling the rolls, brush them with butter and sprinkle with the Parmesan-ranch mix. Bake according to recipe directions. While the rolls are baking, combine the remaining ranch dressing mix with ¾ cup milk and ¾ cup mayonnaise and serve with the rolls.

Stuffed Pizza Rolls

Kids and adults alike will gobble up this fun food that can be served either as a meal or an appetizer. Whether you fill them with pepperoni and cheese or grilled chicken, spinach, and artichoke hearts, be prepared for instant popularity.

1 roll refrigerated pizza dough (or use the recipe for Breadstick Dough on p. 30)

1½ cups shredded mozzarella cheese

Pizza toppings of your choice like ham, pepperoni, chicken, olives, peppers, onion, pineapple, etc.

1 tablespoon olive oil or melted butter

½ teaspoon garlic powder

1 teaspoon dried Italian seasoning

2 tablespoons canned grated Parmesan cheese

Marinara, Pizza Sauce (p. 155), or Guiltless Alfredo Sauce (p. 158)

1. Preheat the oven to the heat specified on pizza dough package or recipe.

2. Unroll your pizza dough onto a lightly floured surface. Pat or roll the dough so it's about 12 x 8 inches. Use a pizza wheel to cut the dough into 24 squares.

3. Place desired toppings (except sauce; reserve that for dipping) in the center of each square and top with about 1 tablespoon shredded cheese, making sure you'll be able to completely enclose the filling with the dough.

4. When all of your dough squares have cheese and toppings on them, carefully lift up each square and wrap the dough around the toppings. Pinch to make sure each ball is sealed shut and then place them seam-side down in a lightly sprayed pie pan (or similar sized dish).

5. Brush the tops of the dough balls with olive oil or melted butter and then sprinkle with the garlic and Italian seasoning and top with Parmesan cheese. You can also replace the garlic, Italian seasoning, and Parmesan with the Garlic Bread Seasoning on p. 53.

6. Place the pan in the preheated oven and bake for about 15–20 minutes or until golden brown on top, checking on them every few minutes after 10 minutes.

7. Serve immediately with warmed marinara sauce, Pizza Sauce (p. 155), or Guiltless Alfredo Sauce (p. 158) on the side for dipping.

Thai Peanut Noodles

This sweet and spicy dish is one of our most popular recipes! Serve it in bistro bowls with chopsticks and you'll feel just like you're at a restaurant.

Serves 4–6

⊕ **Quick and Easy**
🌿 **Vegetarian**

ROLLOVERS
Chicken broth
Green onions
Frresh cilantro

8 ounces Udon or linguine noodles

½ cup chicken broth

3 tablespoons creamy peanut butter

1–2 teaspoons Sriracha chili sauce (1 is mild with a bite, 1½ is medium-hot, and 2 is hot)

1½ tablespoons honey

3 tablespoons soy sauce

1½ tablespoons minced fresh ginger

2–3 cloves garlic, pressed or minced

Chopped green onions

Chopped cilantro

Chopped peanuts

2 limes, cut into quarters, for garnish

1. Cook noodles in salted water according to package directions.

2. While the noodles are cooking, combine the chicken broth, peanut butter, chili sauce, honey, soy sauce, ginger, and garlic in a small saucepan over medium-low heat. Whisk until smooth and remove from heat.

3. Toss cooked noodles with sauce and divide among 4 bowls. Sprinkle with green onions, cilantro, and chopped peanuts, and garnish each serving with 2 lime quarters. Before eating, squeeze lime juice over noodles and stir to combine.

●●●●●●●●●●●●●●●

TIP: Although this dish is hearty, rich, and cheesy, if you cut it into 12 pieces, each piece has only 250 calories!

SERVING SUGGESTION:
Serve with Breadsticks (p. 30) or French Bread (p. 32) and a fresh garden salad.

Peter's Lasagna

This is Kate's brother-in-law's famous lasagna recipe, straight from Italy. Try the sauce with bowtie pasta, mozzarella, freshly grated Parmesan, and bake it until the cheese is bubbly.

1 recipe Peter's Pasta Sauce (facing page)

1 recipe Béchamel Sauce (facing page)

8 ounces shredded mozzarella cheese, divided

1 (16-ounce) container ricotta cheese

4 ounces shredded fresh Parmesan cheese

1 egg, lightly beaten

12 no-boil lasagna noodles

1. Preheat oven to 350 degrees F.

2. Combine the pasta sauce with the Béchamel sauce.

3. Combine 6 ounces mozzarella (about 1¾ cup), ricotta, Parmesan, and the beaten egg.

4. Using a ladle that measures ½ cup (or a ½ cup measuring cup), spread 1 cup of sauce onto the bottom of a 9 x 13-inch pan. Add 3 noodles. Spread a layer of the cheese mixture. Spread 1½ cups sauce and repeat so you have 4 layers of noodles. You should end with a layer of sauce on top. Sprinkle with remaining mozzarella (and some extra Parmesan if you have some left over).

5. Cover tightly with foil and bake about 50 minutes.

6. Remove from the oven and remove the foil. It will probably look a little runny. Don't be scared—you still need to let it stand about 15–20 minutes. During that time, it will thicken up nicely. Cut into 12 pieces and serve.

Peter's Pasta Sauce

½ pound ground beef or Italian sausage

1 onion, chopped

5–6 cloves of garlic, minced or pressed

2 (15-ounce) cans Italian-style diced tomatoes

1 (15-ounce) can tomato sauce

1 zucchini, chopped or shredded

2 carrots, peeled and chopped into small pieces

2 stalks celery, chopped

2 teaspoons sugar

About ¼ teaspoon baking soda (this neutralizes the acid)

Salt and pepper to taste

1. In a large saucepan or skillet with a lid, brown ground beef or sausage, onions, and garlic until meat is cooked and onions are tender.

2. Add the remaining ingredients to the cooked meat, stir, and bring to a simmer. Cover, turn heat to low, and simmer for an hour, stirring occasionally. After an hour, remove from heat and serve over pasta or use in lasagna.

Béchamel Sauce

¼ cup real butter, no substitutes

¼ cup white flour

2½ cups milk

To prepare the Béchamel sauce, melt butter over medium-low heat in a medium saucepan. When melted, whisk in flour until combined. Slowly add milk, whisking constantly. Heat until bubbly and thickened to a medium consistency. To test the consistency, dip the back of a spoon in the sauce and then run your finger through it. If your finger leaves a clear track, the sauce is ready.

Chicken Cacciatore

Tender bites of chicken, mushrooms, and green peppers fill out this rich, savory tomato-based sauce that has a hint of sweetness. Serve over pasta or hot rice.

Serves 6–8

🍲 **Slow Cooker**

ROLLOVERS
Chicken broth
Mushrooms

●●●●●●●●●●●●●●●●●

TIP: A quick way to test the temperature of cooking oil is to flick a few drops of water into it. If nothing happens, wait a few more minutes for the oil to continue warming up. If oil splatters everywhere, turn the heat down, wait a minute, and try again. But if it sizzles, it's the perfect temperature for adding your food!

SERVING SUGGESTION:
Serve with tossed green salad and Breadsticks (p. 30) or French Bread (p. 32).

SLOW COOKER INSTRUCTIONS: Follow recipe directions through step 3, but place the ingredients in a slow cooker instead of a stockpot. Cook on high for 4 hours or on low for 7–8 hours. Add the mushrooms and peppers during the last 30 minutes of cooking. When the mushrooms and peppers are tender, remove the bay leaf and serve over hot linguine or rice.

½ cup olive oil

1 onion, roughly chopped

5–6 cloves garlic, peeled and either crushed or halved

¼ cup white flour

1½ teaspoons kosher salt, divided

1 teaspoon freshly ground black pepper

1 pound boneless skinless chicken breasts or chicken breasts and thighs, trimmed of fat and cut into bite-sized pieces

1 cup apple juice or white grape juice

1 tablespoon white wine vinegar

1½ cups chicken broth

1 (6-ounce) can tomato paste

¼ teaspoon thyme

¼ teaspoon marjoram

1 bay leaf

1 cup sliced mushrooms

1 medium green bell pepper, chopped (about 1 cup)

1 (16-ounce) package linguine, cooked per instructions

Freshly grated Parmesan cheese, to taste

1. Heat olive oil in skillet over medium heat. When the oil is hot, add the onions and garlic and stir frequently until onions are tender and garlic is fragrant. Remove with a slotted spoon (this is why you need to keep the onion and garlic pieces big) and transfer the onions and garlic to your blender. Increase the heat on the stove top to medium-high.

2. In a large zip-top bag, combine flour, 1 teaspoon salt, and black pepper. Add chicken pieces, seal bag, and shake to coat pieces with flour. Place all the chicken from the bag into the hot pan and stir quickly to prevent pieces from sticking together. Sauté until chicken is golden. Remove the chicken with slotted spoon and drain on a paper towel. Remove the pan from heat.

3. While the chicken is draining, add the juice, vinegar, chicken broth, tomato paste, thyme, and marjoram to the onions and garlic in the blender. Blend until smooth. Place the chicken and bay leaf in a medium or large stockpot and pour the blended mixture over the chicken. Cover and simmer over low heat, stirring occasionally, for 60–90 minutes.

4. During the last 15 minutes of cooking, add the mushrooms and green peppers. When the mushrooms and peppers are tender, remove the bay leaf and serve over hot linguine or rice and garnish with Parmesan cheese if desired.

FREEZER INSTRUCTIONS:
Complete steps through browning the chicken. Instead of placing chicken in a stockpot or slow cooker, place it in a freezer-safe container and cover with sauce. When ready to cook, place the frozen mixture in your slow cooker and cook on high for 4–5 hours. You can either cut the mushrooms and peppers ahead of time and freeze them separately from the chicken and sauce or you can just plan to have those in your fridge when you're ready to make this.

Pesto Pasta with Roasted Tomatoes

Light and easy, this pasta dish comes together in a matter of minutes, making it perfect for busy weeknights.

Makes 4 main dish servings or 6 side dish servings

☺ **Quick and Easy**

🌿 **Vegetarian**

ROLLOVER
Parmesan cheese

●●●●●●●●●●●●●●●●●

VARIATION: Add Guiltless Alfredo Sauce (p. 158) to taste for a creamier dish.

1 pint cherry or grape tomatoes

8 ounces mushrooms, sliced (about 3 cups)

3–4 tablespoons extra-virgin olive oil

Kosher salt

Freshly ground black pepper

8 ounces farfalle or bowtie pasta (a little more than 3 cups)

¼ cup pine nuts

½ cup pesto (make your own on p. 47)

⅓ cup freshly shredded Parmesan cheese

1. Preheat oven to 425 degrees F. Bring a large pot of water to boil.

2. Place tomatoes and mushrooms on a foil-lined baking sheet and drizzle with olive oil. Toss with your fingers, making sure everything is coated with olive oil. Sprinkle lightly with kosher salt and freshly ground pepper. Cook for 12–15 minutes or until tomatoes look plump and some of the skins just start to split.

3. When the water comes to a boil, add 2 teaspoons kosher salt and pasta to the water and cook according to package directions.

4. While the pasta is cooking, place the pine nuts in a small skillet over medium heat. Stir frequently until the nuts turn golden brown and look slightly glossy, about 7–9 minutes.

5. To assemble, toss the hot drained pasta with pesto and Parmesan cheese. Top with tomatoes and mushrooms and sprinkle with toasted pine nuts and additional Parmesan cheese if desired.

⊕ **Quick and Easy**

🌿 **Vegetarian**

ROLLOVERS
Spinach
Feta cheese
Mushrooms

Spinach and Feta Pasta

This is Kate's favorite quick and easy weeknight meal. White mushrooms are sautéed until tender with olive oil, garlic, and minced onions and tossed with pasta, tangy feta cheese, and tomatoes for a fresh, healthy, quick meal that is also vegetarian.

8 ounces penne pasta (Don't use ziti—you want the ridges on the penne to "grip" the sauce)

1–2 tablespoons extra-virgin olive oil

1 onion, finely chopped

5–6 cloves garlic, minced or pressed

1 loose cup chopped fresh mushrooms

3 cups fresh spinach (you don't even have to chop it!)

1 (28-ounce) can diced tomatoes

4 ounces feta cheese, crumbled

Kosher salt and freshly ground pepper to taste

1. Bring a large pot of salted water to a boil and add pasta. Cook according to package directions.

2. While the pasta is cooking, heat 1–2 tablespoons of olive oil in a skillet over medium heat. Add onion, garlic, and mushrooms and cook until tender. Add spinach and cook until wilted. Add tomatoes, heat through, and then add drained pasta and crumbled feta. Season with salt and pepper to taste. Heat through and serve; you can crumble a little extra feta on top if desired.

Tomato-Artichoke Pasta

Even though this recipe uses canned tomatoes, it tastes light and fresh. It's the perfect complement to heartier pastas like cheese-filled tortellini.

Serves 4–6

⊙ **Quick and Easy**
🌿 **Vegetarian**

ROLLOVER
Green onions

●●●●●●●●●●●●●●●

SERVING SUGGESTION:
Serve with Breadsticks (p. 30) and a tossed green salad

1 package fresh, filled pasta (like tortel-lini, ravioli, etc.)

1–2 tablespoons extra-virgin olive oil

5–6 cloves garlic, pressed

½ cup chopped green onions

6–7 ounces marinated artichoke hearts, drained and chopped

1 (15-ounce) can diced tomatoes

3 ounces tomato paste

3 ounces apple juice

1 tablespoon balsamic vinegar

½ teaspoon kosher salt

¼ teaspoon black pepper

1. Boil pasta in salted water, according to package instructions.

2. In a large saucepan, heat 1–2 tablespoons of olive oil over medium heat. When the oil is hot, add garlic, green onions, and artichoke hearts. Sauté until the garlic is fragrant. Add tomatoes, tomato paste, apple juice, vinegar, salt, and pepper. Heat through and toss with cooked pasta.

ROLLOVERS
Fresh basil
Fresh oregano

TIP: When cooking garlic, it's important to keep an eye on it to make sure it's not getting brown and crispy because it cooks very quickly and can become bitter.

SERVING SUGGESTION:
Chop any leftover oregano, basil, and garlic and add them to softened butter to serve with crusty sourdough bread. Add a tossed green salad.

Lemon-Zucchini Fettuccine

This is one of Sara's favorite summertime meals, when zucchini and herbs are abundant. Fresh and light-tasting, lemon and fresh basil add brightness to this dish. Grilled zucchini and chicken round this out for a meal that is perfect for company you want to impress.

2 large boneless, skinless chicken breasts

2 lemons, divided

¼ cup plus 3 tablespoons olive oil, divided

2 tablespoons red wine vinegar

1 tablespoon kosher salt

2 medium zucchini

Salt and pepper

5–6 cloves garlic

8 ounces fettuccine

Fresh basil (about ½ cup)

Fresh oregano (about ¼ cup) or about 1 tablespoon dried oregano

1 cup grated Parmesan cheese

1. Prepare grill. You could also do this on the stove top in a skillet or a grill pan.

2. Place chicken in a zip-top bag with the juice of one lemon, 2 tablespoons of olive oil, and the red wine vinegar. Seal the bag and gently squish the bag to make sure the ingredients are incorporated and surrounding the chicken. Set aside for 15–30 minutes.

3. In a large pot, bring water with about 1 tablespoon of kosher salt to a boil. While waiting for the water to boil, slice the zucchini in half lengthwise. Drizzle with 1 tablespoon olive oil and sprinkle with salt and pepper.

4. Press or finely mince garlic cloves. In a small saucepan on the stove, place ¼ cup olive oil and add garlic. Turn the burner to medium-low heat. It shouldn't be popping and frying, the oil should just slowly warm, infusing the oil with the garlic and removing that zing fresh garlic has.

5. When the water is boiling, add the pasta.

6. Remove the chicken from the bag and salt and pepper both sides. Place the chicken and zucchini on grill.

7. While the chicken and zucchini are grilling and pasta is boiling, chop herbs and prepare the cheese. Zest both lemons and juice the one that hasn't been juiced.

8. When the zucchini and chicken are done, remove them from the grill. Allow the chicken to stand for 5 minutes and then chop the zucchini and chicken.

9. Reserve about ½ cup of pasta water. Drain the pasta and immediately place in a big bowl. Place the chopped zucchini and chicken on top. Add lemon zest, lemon juice, cheese, herbs, and the garlic-olive oil mixture.

10. Now take some tongs and give everything a big toss. If you feel it needs more moisture, add a little of the pasta water or a little more olive oil.

11. Garnish with a little more Parmesan on top and another squeeze of lemon if you have any left.

Side Dishes

Potatoes

Vegetables

Rice and Beans

Facing page: Stuffed Blue Cheese Potatoes, see page 183

SERVING SUGGESTION:
Serve with steak, chicken, or hamburgers.

Classic Mashed Potatoes

If creating creamy, smooth mashed potatoes has ever baffled you, look no further than these directions! We'll show you how to make classic mashed potatoes as well as some tasty variations, including the pictured Loaded Mashed Potatoes.

3 pounds russet potatoes	¼ cup (plus more if necessary) milk
¼ cup real butter	Salt and freshly ground black pepper

1. Cut the potatoes into uniform ½-inch pieces; this will help them cook quickly.

2. Bring a large pot of salted water to a boil. When the water boils, add the potatoes and cook until very tender. Slightly overcook the potatoes; you want them to start to crumble when pierced with a fork. Undercooked potatoes will become pasty.

3. Drain and place the potatoes in a large mixing bowl. Add the butter and beat with an electric mixer until the butter is melted and incorporated into the potatoes. (Electric mixers will give you the creamiest potatoes.)

4. Slowly add in milk, starting with ¼ cup, until the desired consistency is reached. Season with salt and pepper and serve.

Cheesy Mashed Potatoes

Substitute buttermilk for regular milk and add ½–¾ cup shredded sharp cheddar cheese for a tangy variation.

Roasted Garlic and Parmesan Potatoes

3 pounds russet potatoes	½ teaspoon kosher salt
1 head roasted garlic (see p. 52)	¼ teaspoon black pepper
⅔ cup grated Parmesan cheese	¼ cup milk
6 tablespoons real butter, softened	

Cook the potatoes according to the directions in the Classic Mashed Potatoes. Add remaining ingredients and mix with an electric mixer until desired consistency is reached.

Loaded Mashed Potatoes

3 pounds russet potatoes

¼ cup real butter, softened

½ cup sour cream

½ teaspoon kosher salt

¼ teaspoon freshly ground black pepper

¼ teaspoon garlic powder

½ cup shredded sharp cheddar cheese

¼ cup sliced green onions

6 ounces (½ of a 12-ounce package) bacon, cooked until crisp and crumbled

Cook the potatoes according to the directions in Classic Mashed Potatoes. Whip the potatoes, butter, sour cream, salt, pepper, and garlic powder. Fold in the remaining ingredients by hand. Reserve 2 tablespoons of the bacon to top the potatoes when serving. If desired, add extra cheddar cheese and onions.

Sweet Potato Fries

These crispy, savory and slightly sweet fries are a delicious, healthy alternative to more traditional French fries.

½ teaspoon cumin

½ teaspoon oregano

½ teaspoon coriander

1 teaspoon kosher salt

1 teaspoon parsley

⅛ teaspoon black pepper

1 pound peeled sweet potatoes cut into ¼-inch matchsticks

2 tablespoons extra-virgin olive oil

1. Preheat oven to 425 degrees F.

2. In a small bowl, combine cumin, oregano, coriander, salt, parsley, and pepper.

3. Place the sweet potatoes in a pile directly on a baking sheet and drizzle with olive oil. Use your hands to toss until all pieces are well coated. Sprinkle seasoning mixture on top and toss again with your hands to coat.

4. Arrange sweet potatoes in a single layer so that pieces are not touching each other. Place the pan in the preheated oven and bake for 15 minutes. Use a metal spatula to gently flip fries and then return pan to oven. Cook for an additional 15–20 minutes or until fries are starting to lightly brown and crisp. Remove pan from oven and cool 5 minutes. Serve immediately with Honey-Lime Dip.

Honey-Lime Dip

1 (6-ounce) container plain, low-fat yogurt

1 tablespoon mayonnaise

½ tablespoon honey

1 tablespoon fresh lime juice

¼ teaspoon cumin

⅛ teaspoon oregano

1 teaspoon parsley

½ teaspoon onion powder

½ teaspoon kosher salt

Whisk together all the ingredients and chill until ready to serve.

Roasted Garlic-Rosemary Potatoes

This recipe has become a favorite on our blog because it's easy, gorgeous, and incredibly delicious.

2½ tablespoons extra-virgin olive oil

About 5 cloves of garlic, minced or pressed

2½ tablespoons chopped fresh rosemary (be sure and strip the needles from the stem before chopping them)

2½ tablespoons coarse-grain or Dijon mustard

Coarsely ground black pepper

1½ pounds baby red, fingerling, or other very small potatoes, washed; try to pick the potatoes that are as bite-sized as possible to increase the sauce-to-potato ratio.

Kosher salt

1. Bring a large pot of salted water to a boil. While the water is heating, combine the olive oil, minced garlic, rosemary, mustard, and some black pepper. Set aside.

2. Preheat oven to 425 degrees F. Line a baking sheet with aluminum foil and set aside.

3. When the water is boiling, add the potatoes and boil for about 10 minutes or until they are easily pierced with a fork. Drain, return the potatoes to the pan, and then toss with the mustard mixture.

4. Spread the potatoes out evenly over the baking sheet and sprinkle with kosher salt. Bake for 10–15 minutes or until the skins begin to brown and sizzle.

Serves 6–8

⊕ **Quick and Easy**

🌿 **Vegetarian**

ROLLOVER
Fresh rosemary

●●●●●●●●●●●●●●●●

TIP: You can do the prep work on these potatoes ahead of time to make mealtime easy. After spreading the potatoes on the baking sheet, cover with some plastic wrap and refrigerate for up to 8 hours. When ready to cook, sprinkle the potatoes with some kosher salt and roast the potatoes at 425 degrees F. for about 15–20 minutes.

SERVING SUGGESTIONS:
Serve with Roasted Pork Tenderloin (p. 148) or grilled steaks.

●●●●●●●●●●●●●●●●

SERVING SUGGESTIONS:
Serve with Slow Cooker French Dip
Sandwiches (p. 134), Cheesesteak
Sandwiches (p. 127), or any other dish
that goes well with fries.

VARIATION: Substitute ½ teaspoon freshly ground black pepper, 2¼
teaspoons garlic salt, and ¼ teaspoon
parsley for the spices listed in Oven-
Baked Steak Fries.

Oven-Baked Steak Fries and Fry Sauce

*Your kids will never complain about these family-favorite fries, which are tossed
in seasoned olive oil and baked rather than fried.*

½ teaspoon cumin

1 teaspoon chili powder

1 teaspoon kosher salt

½ teaspoon freshly ground black pepper

2 tablespoons olive oil

4 medium russet potatoes, washed

1. Preheat oven to 400 degrees F. Mix spices in a medium bowl. Add olive
   oil and combine well.

2. Cut the potatoes into 8 wedges each. Add potato wedges to seasonings
   and toss to coat.

3. Lightly crumple some aluminum foil and place it on a baking sheet. Spray
   the foil with nonstick cooking spray and then arrange potato wedges on
   foil. This makes cleanup easy because your potatoes won't stick, and it
   also ensures that they're cooked evenly.

4. Bake for about 40 minutes.

Fry Sauce

¼ cup real mayonnaise (no Miracle Whip!)

¼ cup ketchup

2–3 teaspoons dill pickle relish

Whisk to combine and serve with fries if desired.

Stuffed Blue Cheese Potatoes

This twist on twice-baked potatoes has been gracing the holiday table at Sara's house since she was a child. It uses blue cheese rather than the classic cheddar. The blue cheese just adds a little more zip than you normally get with cheddar, so even if you think you don't like blue cheese, we bet you'll love these!

Serves 8

ROLLOVERS
Blue cheese
Buttermilk

●●●●●●●●●●●●●●●

TIP: Rubbing the skin of potatoes with shortening or vegetable oil helps make the skin crispy.

SERVING SUGGESTION:
These potatoes pair really well with beef dishes; try serving them with burgers, steaks, or Slow Cooker French Dip Sandwiches (p. 134).

4 medium russet potatoes

1–2 tablespoons shortening or vegetable oil, for rubbing on the potatoes

¼ cup real butter, cut into chunks

½ cup sour cream

1 ounce (¼ cup) crumbled blue cheese

¼ cup milk or buttermilk

¾ teaspoon salt

Dash of pepper

½ teaspoon garlic powder

8 pieces bacon, cooked crisp and crumbled

Shredded cheddar cheese

1. Preheat oven to 400 degrees F. Wash and dry potatoes. Rub them lightly with a bit of shortening or vegetable oil and place directly on oven rack. Bake for one hour or until potatoes are tender when pierced with a fork.

2. Remove potatoes and allow them to cool for 5–10 minutes. Cut an opening on the top and hollow out each potato, or cut each potato in half (as shown in photos) to make 8 servings. You may want to hold them with a potholder as they will still be hot!

3. Scoop out the insides and place in a bowl. Mash, and add butter, sour cream, blue cheese, milk, salt, pepper, and garlic powder. Beat with a hand mixer until fluffy. Carefully spoon mixture back into potato shells. Place in a baking dish.

4. Return the potatoes to the hot oven and bake for 12–15 minutes.

5. Remove, sprinkle bacon and cheddar cheese over each potato, and bake an additional 3–5 minutes or until cheese is melted and bubbly.

TIP: These can also be cooked in the oven at 400 degrees F. for about 15–20 minutes (just check on them to see how they're doing) or in a Panini press for about the same amount of time.

SERVING SUGGESTION:
Serve with Grilled Corn on the Cob (p. 196), cubes of watermelon (see p. 16), and Baby Back Ribs (p. 144) for a perfect summer meal.

Grilled Potatoes and Onions

Smoked paprika adds a smoky, outdoor cooking flavor to these potatoes. Cook them on your grill while making ribs or hamburgers or cook them in your oven or even a Panini press.

Heavy duty aluminum foil

1 potato per person (you can use any kind, but red or Yukon Gold are amazing)

½ small onion per person

1 tablespoon butter per person, cut into pieces

¼ teaspoon kosher salt per person

A few turns of freshly ground black pepper

¼ teaspoon smoked paprika per person

1. Tear sheets (1 per person) of aluminum foil into about 16-inch pieces. Fold each in half and set aside.

2. Preheat grill. Slice potatoes into pieces about ⅛–¼-inch thick and slice onions about ⅛-inch thick.

3. Place 1 potato in the middle of each foil square and dot with butter pieces. Sprinkle with salt and pepper and then sprinkle generously with smoked paprika. Remember, paprika is super mild, so it's hard to add too much. Top each pile with onions.

4. Fold edges in and secure tightly. It's important to get a good seal because the moisture will cook the potatoes and onions and you want all those yummy juices, so if it seems like there's not quite enough foil, wrap packet in another layer.

5. Turn heat on grill to low. Place each packet on the grill. Close lid for 15 minutes. Turn and allow to cook for another 15 minutes. Remove from heat and place packets on a platter for serving (just let people grab their own packets).

☆ **Make Ahead**

TIP: You can assemble the bundles, cover them tightly, and refrigerate them for 1–2 days before serving.

SERVING SUGGESTION:
These beans are perfect with ham on Easter Sunday.

Bacon-Wrapped Green Bean Bundles

These perfectly portioned servings of green beans are wrapped in bacon and drizzled with a warm, sweet and tangy sauce. Gorgeous presentation makes these perfect for a fancy meal, but they're easy to make and can be partially made ahead of time.

1 pound green beans with the ends snapped off (buy or pick about 1½ pounds so you'll have 1 pound after the ends have been snapped)

8 slices lean, regularly sliced bacon

3 tablespoons real butter (no substitutions!)

1 tablespoon minced red, yellow, or white onion

1–2 cloves garlic, minced

1 tablespoon rice vinegar

1 tablespoon granulated sugar

¼ teaspoon kosher salt

A few turns of freshly ground black pepper

1. Bring a large pot of lightly salted water to a boil.

2. If you're using fresh green beans, wash and snap the ends off. Discard any sickly looking, overly skinny, or limp beans.

3. When the water is boiling, briefly boil (blanch) the beans for 2–3 minutes or until you start hearing a popping noise and the beans have turned bright green. Quickly drain and rinse the beans in cold water until they have cooled.

4. Preheat your oven to 400 degrees F.

5. On a cookie sheet, divide the green beans evenly into 8 piles. Carefully wrap each pile of beans with one slice of bacon and return to the baking sheet.

6. Place the pan in the preheated oven and bake for 15–20 minutes or until the bacon is crisp and sizzling.

7. While the bundles are in the oven, melt the butter over medium-high heat in a small saucepan. When the butter is bubbly, add in the onions and garlic and sauté for 2–3 minutes or until the onions are softened and fragrant. Reduce heat to low and add in vinegar, sugar, and salt. Remove from heat and set aside.

8. When ready to serve, place bean bundles on a serving platter and drizzle with sauce. Serve immediately.

Caramelized Green Beans

This is our go-to vegetable side dish that even non-veggie eaters will love!

SERVING SUGGESTION:
We love this with Bacon-Wrapped Teriyaki Chicken Skewers (p. 117) and Lime-Cilantro Rice with Pineapple (p. 204).

6 ounces bacon

1⅛ pounds fresh green beans or 1 pound frozen green beans (not French-style)

2 tablespoons sugar

2 tablespoons soy sauce

½ teaspoon kosher salt

½ red onion, sliced

3–4 cloves garlic, minced or pressed

1 tablespoon olive oil

Lots of freshly ground pepper

1. Begin frying the bacon in a large skillet. Start boiling a large pot of water. Place fresh beans in a colander and rinse them well. Then snap the ends off and snap them in half. Set aside.

2. Prepare the sauce by mixing sugar, soy sauce, and salt in a small bowl. Set aside.

3. Make sure your onions are sliced, your garlic is pressed or minced, and all your ingredients are close to your stove top and ready to go.

4. Remove bacon from pan and drain on a paper towel. If you feel like it, you can crumble it now or wait until it's cooled off a little. Discard all but 2 tablespoons of bacon grease.

5. Add 1 tablespoon olive oil to the bacon grease and increase the heat to medium-high. When the pan is hot, add the onions and garlic. Give them a quick stir.

6. Add the beans to the boiling water. Place a colander in a clean sink. Boil for 1 minute (2–3 minutes if you're using frozen beans); you're not cooking them until they're done, just blanching them to take the edge off. Meanwhile, stir the onions and garlic so they don't scorch. When the beans are bright green, drain them in the colander in the sink.

7. Add the drained beans to the onions and garlic. Stir-fry 2–3 minutes more.

8. Give your sauce a quick whisk and then pour on top of the beans. Keep stir-frying until the beans become a little glazed, or about 2–3 minutes.

9. Add the crumbled bacon and lots of freshly ground pepper to the beans. Keep stir-frying until the sauce sticks to the beans and the bacon.

10. Transfer to a serving dish and allow to stand a few minutes so the beans cool down a bit and the glaze thickens up a little.

Fire-Roasted Artichokes

Steamed artichokes may be delicious, but artichokes roasted over a fire are amazing! Dip them in our Garlic-Herb Sandwich Spread (p. 49) for a perfect appetizer or snack.

●●●●●●●●●●●●●●●●

SERVING SUGGESTION:
Artichokes are perfect alongside your favorite steak.

Prepped artichokes (see tutorial below)

Olive oil

Kosher salt and freshly ground black pepper

Garlic-Herb Sandwich Spread (p. 49) or your favorite dipping sauce for artichokes

1. Preheat grill to medium.

2. Brush both sides of the prepped artichoke with olive oil and sprinkle with kosher salt and pepper.

3. Place the seasoned artichokes on the preheated grill, center side-up. Grill with the lid closed for about 10 minutes and then flip so the center is on the grill grates. Continue grilling for another 5–10 minutes until you have nice grill marks and the flesh appears soft.

How to Prep an Artichoke

1. Remove stem. Just snip the stem so it's about an inch long.

2. Trim the bracts. The bracts are the pointy ends of the leaf-looking things; they are sharp and poky, so just take a pair of kitchen shears (or a clean pair of scissors) and snip the tips all the way around.

3. Cut the top. This step is optional, but if you want, you can take a sharp knife and just cut off the very top. We think it looks prettier when sliced in half, but that's your call!

4. Steam. At this point your artichoke is ready for steaming. Even if you're grilling your artichokes, you still need to steam them first. Bring to boil a couple inches of water in a pot with a steamer insert (a mesh strainer will work if you're in a pinch); place artichokes in stem-side up and cover pot with a lid. If you are going to eat your artichokes just steamed then they'll need to stay in there for anywhere from 30–60 minutes depending on the size. When cooked, the leaves should peel off easily and you should be able to pierce the stem with a fork. If you're roasting them, just steam them for 20 minutes and then remove and allow to cool until they're easy to handle.

5. Slice artichoke in half.

6. Remove the choke. That funny-looking furry thing is the choke. This part is pretty easy because artichokes are kind of color-coded to show you what to do! All of that purple stuff needs to come out. Then just cut as the picture shows to make removing the choke easier. Note that these parts of the artichoke are not edible. Also, the parts that you're removing are not the heart.

After you make that slice shown, just use a spoon to scoop it all out. It should come out fairly easily. Now you're ready to eat them or roast them!

Garlic-Balsamic Asparagus

You can either cook this asparagus in the oven or over the fire on the grill, but either way, it's quick, easy, and delicious!

Serves 4–6

⊕ **Quick and Easy**

🌿 **Vegetarian**

●●●●●●●●●●●●●●●●●

TIP: It might seem wasteful to throw away the woody stems of the asparagus, but they're so tough that no one will eat them anyway; in fact, toughness is one of the biggest reasons people think they don't like asparagus.

SERVING SUGGESTION: Serve with grilled steaks.

VARIATION: Prepare grill to medium-high heat, or about 425 degrees F. Reduce heat to low, lightly oil grill, and place seasoned asparagus perpendicular to the grate of the grill. Drizzle any remaining oil/vinegar mix over the asparagus. Grill for 8–10 minutes or until asparagus is bright green and still slightly crisp, turning very frequently.

1 pound asparagus	1 tablespoon olive oil
½ teaspoon kosher salt	1 tablespoon balsamic vinegar
¼ teaspoon freshly ground black pepper	1 teaspoon minced or pressed garlic

1. Preheat oven to 425 degrees F.

2. Wash asparagus and then snap the woody ends (about 2–3 inches) off the bottom of each stem.

3. In a small bowl, combine salt, pepper, oil, vinegar, and garlic. Drizzle over asparagus and toss to coat.

4. Line a baking sheet with aluminum foil and spray with nonstick cooking spray. Arrange the asparagus in a single layer on the baking sheet. Drizzle any remaining oil and vinegar mixture over the asparagus.

5. Roast for 10 minutes, turning once.

Oven-Roasted Tomatoes

If you're wondering what you're going to do with all those extra tomatoes from your garden or friends' gardens, wonder no more. These tomatoes can be frozen whole, or puréed and used like tomato paste. No matter what you use them for, your house will smell amazing while the tomatoes are roasting!

2 pounds tomatoes, any variety

4 tablespoons extra-virgin olive oil, divided

2 tablespoons minced garlic

1 teaspoon kosher salt

¼ teaspoon fresh, coarsely ground black pepper

1½ teaspoons sugar

1. Preheat oven to 325 degrees F. and line a rimmed cookie sheet with foil.

2. Cut your tomatoes. If you're using small grape or Roma tomatoes, just cut them in half. If you're using anything larger, quarter them.

3. Place the cut tomatoes on prepared baking sheet and drizzle with 3 tablespoons olive oil. Toss with hands until all tomatoes are well coated and then arrange in a single layer, skin sides down.

4. Sprinkle minced garlic over the tomatoes, being careful to let most of it drop directly on the tomatoes. Sprinkle evenly with salt, pepper, and sugar. Finally, drizzle remaining tablespoon of oil over the tomatoes.

5. Place the sheet of tomatoes in the oven and cook for 2½–3 hours, or until the juices have dried up and some of the tomatoes start to brown around the edges. Leftover tomatoes can be frozen whole in a zip-top bag or puréed and frozen in individual 3- or 6-ounce portions (like tomato paste).

Serving size varies

☆ **Make Ahead**

●●●●●●●●●●●●●●●●

TIP: Try substituting the purée for tomato paste, chopping the tomatoes and adding them to dressings or dishes that call for sun-dried tomatoes such as pastas and soups, or slicing them and adding them to sandwiches. They also make great appetizers when placed on baguette slices with a soft, spreadable cheese. You can't go wrong eating them right off the pan either!.

Grilled Stuffed Zucchini

Grill up your garden's summer bounty in this healthy, hearty meal!

Makes 4 main dish servings or 12 appetizer or side dish servings

●●●●●●●●●●●●●●●●●

TIP: These can be cooked indoors on an indoor grill pan or the broiler of your oven. If you cook these on an indoor grill pan, cooking will take a little longer since you can't close the lid to keep in the heat. Either way, finishing them under the broiler will add some brownness and crispiness.

SERVING SUGGESTION:

Serve this as a main dish with a green salad and some crusty bread or cut them into thirds for a side dish or appetizer.

2 medium zucchini (about 10 inches long)

½ tablespoon extra-virgin olive oil

Kosher salt and black pepper to season

4 ounces Italian turkey sausage

¼ cup diced red onion

2 cloves garlic, minced

1 medium tomato, diced (about ½ cup)

1½ tablespoons chopped fresh basil or 1 teaspoon dried basil

¼ teaspoon kosher salt

⅛ teaspoon black pepper

⅔ cup prepackaged Italian cheese blend, plus 2 tablespoons for garnish

1 tablespoon Italian-style bread crumbs, plus 1 teaspoon for garnish

1. Slice the zucchini in half lengthwise. Be sure to leave the ends on.

2. Scoop out the centers, saving them in a bowl. Leave at least ¼ inch around the edges and bottoms. Sort out ½ cup of the best parts of the scooped-out zucchini (avoiding the seeds, if possible), dice, and set aside. This will go in your filling.

3. Drizzle the zucchini shells with a little olive oil and use your hands to rub it on all sides. Sprinkle with some kosher salt and black pepper and set aside.

4. Preheat grill to medium.

5. Remove the sausage from the casings. Brown the sausage until you no longer see pink. Add the onion, garlic, and diced zucchini. Cook for 2–3 minutes, or until onion is tender. Add the tomato, basil, salt, and black pepper. Remove from heat and set aside.

6. Place the zucchini hollow-side down on the grill. Grill for about 5 minutes on medium heat. They should have nice grill marks and look tender on the inside. Remove from heat.

7. Add the cheese and bread crumbs to filling mixture. Stir to combine and then divide the filling between the zucchini. Top each zucchini with about 1 tablespoon cheese and sprinkle with ¼–½ teaspoon bread crumbs. Lastly, give them a little drizzle of extra-virgin olive oil.

8. Place them back on the grill filling-side up. Close the grill lid and cook for another 5–7 minutes. Larger and thicker zucchini will take a few minutes longer to cook.

How to Grill Corn on the Cob

GENERAL TIPS

1. If possible, soak the corn in cool water for at least 30 minutes, particularly if you're placing the corn directly on the grill or cooking in the husks.

2. Leave the stem on the cob—it creates a nice handle to use to turn the corn while it's cooking and is great for kids to hold onto when eating their corn.

3. If you have an upper rack on your grill, use it for grilling the corn. While your meat is cooking below, the corn can cook happily up top and you won't have to be so vigilant about keeping an eye on it.

The Foil Method

This method is probably the best for beginners because you don't have to be quite as careful with it. Also, it's a great way to add flavored butters. Soaking the corn is recommended but not necessary for this method.

1. Remove the husks and silk from the corn, wash it, and dry it. Lay the clean corn cob on a piece of heavy-duty aluminum foil. If you don't have heavy duty, make sure to layer a few sheets of regular foil together or you run the risk of burning the corn.

2. Rub some real, softened butter all over the surface of the corn cob. Sprinkle with kosher salt and freshly ground pepper. You can add in any seasonings or fresh herbs you like at this point.

3. Securely seal the foil on both ends and the top. You will rotate the corn so you want to make sure it's sealed up tight so the butter doesn't leak out.

4. Place on grill preheated to medium and rotate every 5–10 minutes for about 15–20 minutes. Be careful when opening—it will release hot steam.

Directly on the Grill

This method is delicious, but it requires vigilance to make sure the corn doesn't overcook. Be sure to soak the corn before grilling or the kernels will shrivel up!

1. Lightly brush (or spray) olive oil over clean corn cobs. Use your hands to make sure it's well-coated.

2. Sprinkle the corn with salt, pepper, and desired seasonings.

3. Place the corn directly on the grill with medium heat and turn often. The kernels will brighten in color and then caramelize. When you see golden brown spots, it's probably done. It usually takes only about 10 minutes, 15 if you're cooking the corn on a lower heat or on the upper rack of the grill.

In the Husk

This method is a little work-intensive because you have to remove the silk and then re-husk the corn. However, the husks keep the corn moist while allowing the smoke from the grill to flavor the corn.

1. Carefully pull down the outer corn husks, leaving them attached to the corn cob.

2. Remove the stringy silk and then carefully place the husks back up onto the corn cob.

3. If you like, use a longer piece of husk to secure the rest of the husks to the cob.

4. Be sure to soak your corn for at least 30 minutes in cool water before proceeding to the next step.

5. Place directly on grill (again, upper rack works well to avoid burning, or place it on the outer edge of the grill where it's not so hot).

6. Turn every few minutes until corn kernels brighten in color and appear plump, or for about 15 minutes. When the corn is cooked, slather on the butter and sprinkle with salt and pepper.

⊕ **Quick and Easy**

ROLLOVER
Cotija cheese

●●●●●●●●●●●●●●●●●●

TIP: Cotija cheese is a soft, tangy crumbling cheese usually found in the grocery store near the cream cheese and fresh Parmesan cheese. You can also try using queso fresco, Parmesan, or feta cheese.

SERVING SUGGESTIONS:
Serve with Grilled Taco Chicken (p. 114) or Chili-Lime Steak (p. 124).

Mexican-Style Corn on the Cob

This common Mexican street food is known as "elote" south of the border. Buy corn when it's sweetest (and least expensive!) for this Mexican treat.

4 ears fresh corn on the cob

1 cup shredded Cotija cheese (see tip about Cotija cheese)

3 tablespoons mayonnaise

2 tablespoons sour cream

¼–½ teaspoon lime zest

½ teaspoon fresh lime juice

¼ teaspoon chili powder

¼ teaspoon cayenne pepper, optional

Pinch of kosher salt

1 lime, cut into 4 wedges

1. Cook your corn as desired. We highly recommend grilling it (see p. 196), but you can boil it if it's more convenient.

2. Using a fine cheese grater such as a microplane, grate the cheese onto a plate big enough to roll the corn around on.

3. Mix the mayonnaise and sour cream in a small bowl. Add the lime zest and juice. Whisk in the chili powder, cayenne, and salt. Set aside. This part can be made ahead of time and stored in the refrigerator.

4. When the corn is finished cooking and is still hot, spread some of the sauce over the corn. Roll it in the shredded cheese. If desired, sprinkle with a little extra chili powder. Serve immediately with a wedge of lime for squeezing over the corn before eating.

Oven-Roasted Broccoli

Broccoli takes on a whole new flavor and texture when roasted in the oven. You'll be surprised that even picky eaters gobble this up. It's quick and easy and a little different from the norm.

4–5 cups broccoli (about 2 regular-sized heads), cleaned and stems trimmed

3 tablespoons olive oil

½ teaspoon kosher salt

⅛ teaspoon freshly ground black pepper

1–2 tablespoons shredded Parmesan cheese

1. Preheat oven to 425 degrees F.
2. Place broccoli on a foil-lined baking sheet. Drizzle the broccoli with olive oil and then toss to combine and coat each piece. Sprinkle with salt and pepper. Place the baking sheet in oven and bake for 15–20 minutes or until stems are golden brown and slightly crisp looking. Remove broccoli from oven and immediately sprinkle with Parmesan cheese. Toss and serve.

Serves 6–8

☺ **Quick and Easy**

🌿 **Vegetarian**

●●●●●●●●●●●●●●●

VARIATION: For garlicky broccoli, toss in 2 cloves minced garlic before cooking. For a fresh twist, try a squeeze of fresh lemon juice right after it comes out of the oven.

ROLLOVER
Mushrooms

SERVING SUGGESTIONS:
Serve with Natchitoches Meat Pies
(p. 128) or Fauxtisserie Chicken (p. 110).

VARIATION: For quick and easy
Dirty Rice, cook ½ pound of sausage
until it is about halfway done. Add 1
cup chopped green peppers with the
onions. Omit the black pepper and substitute Cajun or Creole seasoning (like
Tony Chachere's) for the salt. Season
with salt and pepper as necessary.

Baked Mushroom Rice

*Beef broth and apple juice add richness to this easy side dish that bakes in the
oven while your hands are busy working on something else. If you want a little
taste of the South, try the variation for Dirty Rice.*

2 tablespoons butter

½ cup onion, chopped

1 cup sliced mushrooms

3 cups beef broth

½ cup apple juice

1 tablespoon white vinegar

¾ teaspoon kosher salt

1 teaspoon freshly ground black pepper

2 cups uncooked long-grain rice

1. Preheat oven to 375 degrees F. Spray a 9 x 13-inch dish with nonstick
   cooking spray and set aside.

2. Melt butter over medium heat. Add chopped onion and cook, stirring frequently, for about 2 minutes. Add mushrooms and continue cooking until
   the onions are translucent and the mushrooms are tender. Remove from
   heat and combine the remaining ingredients in the pan.

3. Transfer the mixture to the prepared 9 x 13-inch dish. Cover tightly with
   aluminum foil and bake for 45–60 minutes or until the liquid is absorbed.
   Stir before serving.

Fried Rice

Serve this fried rice with any tropical or Asian dish. You can also add leftover chicken, ham, shrimp, or scrambled eggs to make it a delicious, easy meal.

Serves 8–10

⊙ **Quick and Easy**

3 tablespoons butter

¼ cup minced red onion

2 tablespoons chopped green onions

1½ teaspoons minced garlic

¼ cup chopped carrots

½ cup chopped mushrooms

8 ounces shredded cabbage or coleslaw mix

4 cups cooked white rice

3–4 generous tablespoons soy sauce

¼ teaspoon celery salt

½ teaspoon dehydrated onion

¼ teaspoon freshly ground black pepper

½ teaspoon kosher salt

½ teaspoon sugar

½ teaspoon granulated garlic

●●●●●●●●●●●●●●●

TIP: Cold rice works best in this recipe, so leftover rice makes this dish even quicker and easier!

SERVING SUGGESTION: This rice is delicious with Spicy Honey Chicken (p. 119).

Heat the butter over medium heat and sauté the onions, garlic, carrots, mushrooms, and cabbage until carrots are tender. Add cooked rice, soy sauce, and seasonings. Serve immediately.

Serves 4 as a main dish and
6–8 as a side dish

⊙ **Quick and Easy**
🌿 **Vegetarian**

ROLLOVER
Chicken broth

●●●●●●●●●●●●●●●●

SERVING SUGGESTIONS:
Serve with Grilled Taco Chicken (p. 114)
or Chili-Lime Steak (p. 124) for a
healthy high-protein meal.

Black Beans

Sara fell in love with black beans while living in Brazil. This is her quick and easy version that can be served as a meatless meal on a busy weeknight or as a side dish for any Latin-American-themed meal.

1 tablespoon olive oil

⅔ cup diced onion

2–3 garlic cloves, pressed or finely minced

2 (15-ounce) cans black beans, drained and rinsed

1 cup chicken broth (or 1 cup water plus 1 teaspoon chicken bouillon)

¼ teaspoon cumin

¼ teaspoon coriander

¼ teaspoon oregano

½ teaspoon salt

¼ teaspoon pepper

Juice of 1 lime

Shredded Monterey Jack or cheddar cheese, for garnish, optional

1. In a large skillet, heat some olive oil over medium-high heat. Sauté the onions for about 3 minutes or until they just start to become translucent. Add garlic and sauté for about 30 seconds more.

2. Add beans, broth, and remaining seasonings and bring to a boil. Reduce heat to low and simmer gently for about 7 minutes, stirring occasionally.

3. When the beans are done cooking, remove from heat and add in the juice of one lime. Using the back of a spoon or rubber spatula, mash about ¼–½ of the beans to thicken the consistency. If you want a soupier consistency, just add a little more broth.

4. To serve, sprinkle each serving with shredded Monterey Jack or cheddar cheese, as desired.

Sweet and Savory Coconut Rice

Serves 8

⊕ **Quick and Easy**
🌿 **Vegetarian**

The coconut flavor in this rice is subtle and slightly tropical. Tossed with green onions and seasoned with salt and pepper, this rice is perfect for mild rice that's just a little bit different.

ROLLOVER
Green onions

2 cups white or jasmine rice

1 (14-ounce) can coconut milk

2 cups water

1 teaspoon kosher salt

Splash of white vinegar

2–3 teaspoons granulated sugar

¼ cup chopped green onions, plus chopped green onion tops

Black pepper to taste

●●●●●●●●●●●●●●●

TIP: Adding vinegar to the water before cooking rice helps keep the grains separated and prevents the rice from becoming overly sticky or mushy.

1. Combine rice, coconut milk, water, salt, vinegar, and sugar in a saucepan and bring to a boil. Turn heat to low and cover for 20 minutes or until most of the liquid is absorbed. Allow to stand 5 minutes. Add chopped green onion bottoms, black pepper (if desired), and additional salt if necessary.

2. Garnish with green onion tops and serve immediately.

SERVING SUGGESTIONS:
Serve with Orange Thai Beef Skewers (p. 121), Indian-Spiced Pork Skewers (p. 150), Bacon-Wrapped Teriyaki Chicken Skewers (p. 117), or any Asian- or tropical-themed dish.

Lime-Cilantro Rice with Pineapple

●●●●●●●●●●●●●●●●

TIP: If you serve the leftovers, you may need to add some additional lime juice to perk up the flavor.

SERVING SUGGESTION:
Serve with any tropical- or Latin-influenced dish including Chili-Lime Steak (p. 124) or Bacon-Wrapped Teriyaki Chicken Skewers (p. 117).

This is our go-to recipe for rice side dishes. It goes well with fresh flavors and food hot from the grill.

1 cup long-grain white rice

2 cups water

2 tablespoons real butter

Juice from 1 large lime

1 (8-ounce) can crushed pineapple, drained

½–¾ cup chopped fresh cilantro

Kosher salt and freshly ground black pepper to taste

1. In a large saucepan, combine rice and water. Bring to a boil over high heat and then reduce heat to low, cover tightly, and cook for 20 minutes. Remove from heat and allow to stand, covered, for 5 minutes, so rice can absorb more water.

2. After 5 minutes, add the butter and stir to melt. Add the lime juice, pineapple, and cilantro. Stir to combine, and then add salt and pepper to taste. Serve immediately.

Louisiana-Style Red Beans and Rice

One of Kate's first meals after she moved to Louisiana was red beans and rice, and that was when she realized that moving there might not be the end of the world. Hearty and filling, homey and comforting, smoky and delicious, this recipe clocks in at around only 220 calories and 4 grams of fat per serving.

Serves 8

🍲 **Slow Cooker**

ROLLOVER
Smoked sausage

●●●●●●●●●●●●●●●●

TIP: Andouille sausage, a Louisiana smoked sausage, is extremely smoky and flavorful, but it can also be quite spicy. Because you're not using much in this recipe, the beans won't be too spicy, but the sausage adds a lot of flavor.

1 pound dry red kidney beans, rinsed and sorted

6 cups water

5 regular bouillon cubes or 1 tablespoon plus 2 teaspoons chicken base

¼ pound smoked sausage (Andouille sausage if you can find it), quartered and cut into thin slices.

1 onion, chopped

4–5 cloves garlic, minced

¾ teaspoon cumin

¾ teaspoon coriander

¾ teaspoon oregano

⅛–¼ teaspoon cinnamon (the secret ingredient)

4 cups water

1 tablespoon vinegar

2 cups long-grain white rice

Add the following if you're not using Andouille sausage:

½–1 teaspoon smoked paprika or liquid smoke

1 teaspoon Cajun or Creole seasoning (Tony Chachere's is inexpensive and easy to find)

1. Combine all ingredients except for the last 3 in a Crock-Pot and cook on high for 4–5 hours or on low all day. You can also cook it on high until it starts to boil and then switch the heat to low.

2. When beans are tender, mash about 85–90 percent of them against the side of the Crock-Pot. Add more seasonings if necessary. Replace lid and turn off heat.

3. In a medium saucepan, bring 4 cups water, vinegar, and rice to a boil. Reduce heat to low, cover, and steam for 20 minutes.

4. Ladle 1 cup of beans into individual bowls and top with ½ cup of rice.

High-Altitude Instructions: Soak the beans overnight in the crock of the slow cooker or in a non-reactive bowl. When ready to cook, rinse the beans and then proceed with the recipe as instructed.

Desserts

Facing page: Pumpkin Cheesecake with Pecan-Gingersnap Crust, see page 230

●●●●●●●●●●●●●●●

TIP: When baking, it's important
to lightly spoon the flour into the
measuring cups and then level with a
knife. It's particularly important in this
recipe; directly scooping out the flour
with a measuring cup will result in dry,
crumbly dough.

Sugar Cookies

*If you're still searching for the perfect sugar cookie recipe, look no further!
When rolled out thick and baked until just golden around the edges, these
cookies are soft and melt-in-your-mouth delicious, but they're also fabulous
rolled thin and baked until golden brown and crispy. For best results, use a
stand mixer for this recipe.*

1 cup real butter (no substitutes!)	3 cups flour
1 cup sugar	1½ teaspoons baking powder
1 egg, extra large	½ teaspoon salt
1½ teaspoons almond extract (you could use vanilla instead)	

1. Cream butter and sugar until light and fluffy, about 2 minutes. Add in egg
   and the extract and mix to incorporate.

2. In a separate bowl, combine flour, baking powder, and salt and whisk to
   combine. Slowly add the flour mixture to the butter mixture and mix until
   completely combined.

3. To make the chilling and cutting process easier, roll the dough ¼-inch
   thick between 2 sheets of parchment paper. Lay the sheet of dough flat
   on a cookie sheet and refrigerate for 30 minutes or place in the freezer for
   15 minutes.

4. Cut cookies in desired shapes. Bake in preheated 350 degree F. oven for
   8–12 minutes on ungreased or parchment-lined baking sheet. For soft
   cookies, bake 8–10 minutes, or until just set. For lightly crisp cookies,
   bake 10–13 minutes, or until the edges are golden brown. If you're
   making large cookies, or ones with small parts or heavy frosting, you will
   want to be careful because they might break when they're super soft.

5. When the desired doneness is reached, allow to cool on the pans for
   about 5 minutes and then transfer to the cooling racks and let the cookies
   cool completely. Decorate as desired.

Jam-Filled Cookies

1 recipe Sugar Cookie dough

Jam, any flavor

4 ounces cream cheese

½ teaspoon almond extract

¼ cup dark or semisweet chocolate chips

¼ teaspoon shortening

1. Prepare cookie dough through Step 3.

2. While dough is chilling, soften the cream cheese in the microwave until it spreads easily. Mix in ½ teaspoon almond flavoring. Preheat oven to 350 degrees F.

3. For the next step, you will need 2 different-sized but matching or coordinating cookie cutters. Cut out an even number of the larger cookie cutter shape. Place half of the cutouts on the cookie sheet and spread with cream cheese. Use the smaller cookie cutter to cut the center out of the remaining cutouts. Carefully place them on top of each cream cheese-covered cutout. Bake for 8–12 minutes or until golden brown on ungreased baking sheet.

4. Remove from oven and allow to cool for 5 minutes and then transfer to a wire rack and allow to cool completely. Gently spread any flavor of jam into the center of each cookie. If desired, melt ¼ cup chocolate chips with ¼ teaspoon shortening in a zip-top bag and knead the bag to combine. Cut a tiny corner off the bag and drizzle the chocolate over the cookies. Allow the chocolate to solidify and serve.

Chocolate Toffee Cookies

1 batch of Sugar Cookies

¾ cup dark or semisweet chocolate chips

1 tablespoon shortening

Toffee bits (like Heath)

Almond bark

1. Bake cookies until they are golden brown and crispy. For best results, place them in an airtight container and freeze for up to 1 week.

2. Combine chocolate and shortening in a microwave-safe bowl. Heat in 30-second increments, stirring in between, until the chocolate is smooth. Dip half of each cookie into the chocolate. Sprinkle with Heath bits and allow to cool on wax paper or parchment. You can speed this up by popping them into the freezer.

3. Place a few squares of almond bark into a zip-top bag and seal. Heat in 30-second increments, kneading the bag in between to make sure the almond bark is melted.

4. Cut a tiny corner off the bag and drizzle the almond bark over the chocolate. Allow to cool until the chocolate is solid and serve.

Gingerbread Cookies

If you think you don't like gingerbread cookies, try this recipe! Your house will smell amazing and you won't be able to help but feel the holiday cheer.

Serving size varies depending on size of cookie cutter used

☆ **Make Ahead**

●●●●●●●●●●●●●●●●

TIP: Try doubling this recipe to have cookies to decorate the Christmas tree or to have available for decorating at a Christmas party.

½ cup butter
½ cup sugar
½ cup molasses
1 egg yolk
2 cups flour
½ teaspoon salt

½ teaspoon baking powder
½ teaspoon baking soda
½ teaspoon cinnamon
1 teaspoon cloves
1 teaspoon ginger
½ teaspoon nutmeg

1. Cream butter and sugar. Add molasses and egg yolk. In a medium bowl, combine remaining ingredients. Add flour mixture to butter mixture. Chill for at least an hour. It's a fairly sticky dough so you might need to chill it a little longer.

2. Preheat oven to 350 degrees F. Roll dough to ¼ inch thick and cut with cookie cutters. Place cookies 2 inches apart on an ungreased or parchment-lined baking sheet. Bake 8–10 minutes. If you bake them on the short end they will stay soft and chewy and if you bake them on the longer end they will be nice and crispy. They're great either way!

3. Allow to cool about 5 minutes on pan and then transfer to wire rack and cool completely. Once they're cooled, decorate as desired.

Peanut Butter and White Chocolate Chip Chocolate Cookies

Makes about 4 dozen cookies

Next time you're craving chocolate chip cookies, try this one instead. This rich chocolate cookie is laced with a combination of both white chocolate chips and peanut butter chips. Great with a tall glass of milk any time of the day.

½ cup butter-flavored shortening

½ cup butter

1 cup brown sugar

1 cup granulated sugar

1½ teaspoons vanilla

2 eggs

2½ cups flour

1 teaspoon baking soda

1 teaspoon baking powder

½ teaspoon salt

6 tablespoons unsweetened cocoa powder

1 cup peanut butter chips

1 cup white chocolate chips

1. Preheat oven to 350 degrees F.

2. Cream together the butter, shortening, brown sugar, and granulated sugar. Add the vanilla and the eggs one at a time.

3. In a separate bowl whisk together the flour, soda, baking powder, salt, and cocoa powder. Add flour mixture to the butter mixture to combine and then mix in the chips.

4. Using a cookie scoop or a spoon, drop onto an ungreased or parchment-lined cookie sheet. Bake for about 8–10 minutes. Allow to cool for about 5 minutes and then transfer to a cooling rack to cool completely.

Apple Streusel Bars

These bars are kind of like apple pie, only better. They're perfect for dessert, particularly for a brunch, but they're also great for a sweet breakfast treat or a late-night snack.

Sweet Pastry

2 cups flour

½ cup sugar

½ teaspoon salt

½ teaspoon baking powder

1 cup real butter, softened, no substitutions

1 egg, beaten

Apple Filling

¼ cup flour

½ cup granulated sugar

1 teaspoon cinnamon

4 cups (about 3 medium) sliced, peeled baking apples (Granny Smith or Gala work beautifully)

Glaze

2 cups powdered sugar

1 teaspoon almond extract

About 3 tablespoons milk (whole milk is best)

1. To prepare the crust, mix flour, sugar, salt, and baking powder in a medium bowl. Cut in butter with a pastry blender or two knives until you have pea-sized crumbles. Gently mix in beaten egg.

2. Spray a 9 x 13-inch baking dish with nonstick cooking spray. Gently pat about ⅔ of the crumb mixture onto the bottom of the dish and set aside. Preheat oven to 350 degrees F.

3. To prepare apple filling, combine flour, sugar, and cinnamon. Toss with apples and spread apples out on prepared crust. Sprinkle reserved crust mixture over apples evenly and bake in preheated oven for 40 minutes. When finished, allow to cool completely.

4. To prepare glaze, whisk together powdered sugar, almond extract, and enough milk to achieve desired consistency. Transfer glaze into a zip-top bag and cut off a very small portion of one of the corners. Drizzle glaze over cooled pastry and allow to harden (you can place it in the freezer to hurry things along). Cut into bars and serve.

Cookie Sundae Cups

⊙ **Quick and Easy**

Known as Pizzookies on our blog, these sweet treats come together in a matter of minutes. You can use your favorite chocolate chip cookie dough recipe or just buy some refrigerated cookie dough. Serve these hot from the oven and topped with a scoop of vanilla ice cream and chocolate and/or caramel syrup.

Chocolate chip cookie dough   Hot Fudge Sauce (p. 252)
Vanilla ice cream   Buttermilk Caramel Sauce (p. 70)

1. Preheat oven to 350 degrees F. Fill ungreased ramekins about ½ full of cookie dough.

2. Bake for about 12–14 minutes or until golden around the edges but still soft in the middle.

3. Remove from the oven and allow to cool about 5 minutes. Top with a scoop of vanilla ice cream and drizzle with caramel and chocolate sauces.

Peanut Butter and Jam Bars

What kid (or kid at heart!) doesn't love PB&J? These bars are Sara's favorite childhood bars, but they'll be well-loved in just about any family.

½ cup butter-flavored shortening

½ cup sugar

½ cup brown sugar

½ cup creamy peanut butter

1 large egg

1 teaspoon vanilla

1¼ cups flour

¾ teaspoon baking soda

½ teaspoon baking powder

¾ cup strawberry or raspberry jam

Glaze

¼ cup real butter, melted

2 cups powdered sugar

1 teaspoon vanilla

2 tablespoons hot water

1. Preheat oven to 350 degrees F.

2. Cream shortening and both sugars together until light and fluffy. Add in peanut butter and combine. Mix in egg and vanilla.

3. Add flour in small amounts at a time while the mixer is running. When about half of the flour is left, whisk the baking soda and baking powder into it. Combine well and then add the remaining flour mixture to the dough mixture and mix until everything is incorporated.

4. Reserve one cup of the dough and set aside. Take the remaining dough and press it into the bottom of an ungreased 9 x 13-inch pan. Spread jam evenly over the dough.

5. Crumble the reserved pieces of dough over the jam. You can also flatten small pieces into small discs and lay them over the jam. Some of the jam will still show through when you're done and that's fine.

6. Bake for 20–30 minutes. The top should be set and just barely golden brown. Don't overcook. When done, remove from oven and cool on a rack. Wait until they are completely cooled to room temperature to glaze.

7. Mix all the glaze ingredients together and whisk until smooth. Spread over cooled bars. Let the glaze set a bit to harden and then cut the bars into squares or triangles.

Pecan Bars

If you love pecan pie but don't want to commit to an entire slice, whip up some of these bars!

☆ **Make Ahead**

6 tablespoons butter

6 tablespoons shortening

¾ cup powdered sugar

1½ cups plus 2 tablespoons flour

2 eggs

1 cup brown sugar

½ teaspoon baking powder

½ teaspoon salt

½ teaspoon vanilla

¾ cup chopped pecans

Glaze

1½ cups powdered sugar

2 tablespoons butter, melted

3 tablespoons orange juice

1 teaspoon lemon juice

1. Preheat oven to 350 degrees F.

2. Cream butter, shortening, and powdered sugar. Add 1½ cups flour and mix until combined. Press evenly in the bottom of a 9 x 13-inch pan. Bake for 13–14 minutes.

3. Mix remaining flour and the rest of the ingredients (except for the glaze ingredients) and spread over the hot crust. Return pan to oven and bake 20 minutes more.

4. Remove from oven. While still warm, spread with glaze. Cool completely and cut into bars.

Strawberry Cheesecake Bars

The cheesecake base for these bars is already to-die-for, but mix in fresh straw-berry sauce, bake it on a pecan shortbread crust, and cut it into easy-to-hold bars and you can't beat it.

1 (16-ounce) package Pecan Sandies Cookies, divided

1½ tablespoons butter, melted

11 ounces cream cheese, softened (not low-fat)

2 eggs

⅔ cup sugar

pinch salt

1½ teaspoons vanilla

½ teaspoon almond extract

2 cups sour cream

1¼ cups Strawberry Sauce (p. 71) or homemade strawberry jam, divided (you can also use bottled strawberry topping or canned strawberry pie filling)

1. Preheat oven to 375 degrees F.

2. Spray a 9 x 13-inch pan with nonstick cooking spray. In a food processor, process ¾ of the Pecan Sandies (reserve 6 cookies). Mix with melted butter and lightly press onto the bottom of the pan. Set aside.

3. In a large bowl or the bowl of a stand mixer, combine cream cheese, eggs, sugar, salt, vanilla, almond extract, and sour cream. Beat on high for 4–5 minutes. Spread half of the cheesecake batter onto the bottom of a 9 x 13-inch pan lightly sprayed with nonstick cooking spray.

4. Pour ¾ cup of the strawberry sauce over the batter, spreading gently to cover the surface (it doesn't have to be perfect). Spread remaining cheesecake batter over the strawberry layer and then spoon remaining ½ cup of strawberry sauce over the batter. Being careful not to cut into the surface of the cookie crust, swirl the strawberry mixture with a butter knife.

5. Bake for 25–35 minutes or until center is jiggly but not liquid. While baking, process remaining 6 cookies. During the last 10 minutes of baking, sprinkle the cookies on top of the cheesecake. Chill for at least 8 hours and cut into squares. If desired, drizzle remaining strawberry sauce over the individual squares.

●●●●●●●●●●●●●●●●

TIP: You can substitute 1 teaspoon of other flavorings such as lemon, orange, cherry, strawberry, etc. for the mint and then change the food coloring accordingly.

Mint Brownies

A specialty of Sara's mom, these decadent, chocolate-glazed, from-scratch brownies are a perfect treat any time of year. Try substituting different flavors such as orange or raspberry extracts in the frosting!

4 (1-ounce) squares unsweetened baking chocolate

1 cup butter

4 eggs

2 cups sugar

1 teaspoon vanilla

1¼ cups flour

½ teaspoon baking powder

Frosting

1–2 tablespoons milk

2 cups powdered sugar

¼ cup butter, softened

1½ teaspoons peppermint extract

Green food coloring

Chocolate Glaze

6 ounces (about 1 cup) semisweet or dark chocolate chips

6 tablespoons real butter

1. Preheat oven to 350 degrees F. Line a 9 x 13-inch pan with foil, making sure the foil extends over the edges by at least one inch. Lightly spray with nonstick cooking spray and set aside.

2. Chop both the unsweetened chocolate and the butter into chunks and place together in a microwave-safe bowl. Microwave in 30-second intervals, stirring in between, until just melted and smooth. Set aside to cool, stirring occasionally.

3. With an electric mixer or stand mixer, beat eggs, sugar, and vanilla for 2 minutes. While the egg mixture is being beaten, measure out the flour and combine with the baking powder. While the mixer is running, slowly add the melted chocolate and beat to combine. Turn the beater speed to low and add in flour by spoonfuls. Mix just until combined. Pour batter into the prepared pan and bake for 20–30 minutes or until a knife poked in center comes out clean.

4. Cool completely on a metal rack. When the brownies have cooled to room temperature, prepare the frosting. Combine all the frosting ingredients, starting with 1½ tablespoons of milk, and beat until light and

fluffy. Add more milk by the teaspoonful as needed. Spread frosting evenly over the brownies and then chill the brownies in the refrigerator.

5. While the brownies are chilling, prepare the chocolate glaze. Place chocolate chips and 6 tablespoons butter in a microwave safe bowl. Microwave in 30-second intervals, stirring in between, until just melted and smooth. Set aside to cool for about 15 minutes and then carefully spread on top of the frosting layer. Return the pan to the fridge to cool. When chocolate has hardened, use the edges of foil to remove the entire sheet of brownies from the pan. Cut into squares and serve.

Christmas Candy Cane Brownies

Use a few drops of red food coloring in the frosting layer and sprinkle crushed peppermint candy canes on the top for a festive holiday treat.

How to Make a Pie Crust

If you're scared of making your own pie crust, you need to try this recipe! It's so quick and easy and yields such light, flaky crust that you'll never go back to refrigerated pie crusts.

Makes 1 9-inch pie crust

1¼ cups all-purpose flour
½ teaspoon salt
⅓ cup plus 1 tablespoon butter-flavored shortening
Ice water (about ¼ cup)

1. Combine flour and salt in a medium-sized bowl. Add shortening in small cubes.

2. Cut in shortening with a pastry blender or 2 table knives until you get pieces that are about pea-sized.

3. Sprinkle the ice water a tablespoon at a time over the flour-shortening mixture. Very, very gently, turn the dough with your fingers so it gets exposed to the water. You're NOT mixing, just trying to moisten all of the flour-shortening mixture. Gradually, all of the flour mixture will be moistened. Gently pat the dough into a ball—it should come together easily but not be sticky. Form the dough into a disc, wrap in plastic wrap, and refrigerate until ready to use.

4. When you're ready to roll out your pie crust, lightly flour your work surface and place the dough ball on the surface. One of the keys in making pie crust is to handle the dough as little as possible. Don't worry too much—this recipe for crust is pretty forgiving—but at the same time, the less you touch it, the more tender and flaky it will be. Starting in the center, roll the dough out into a circle shape, about ⅛-inch thick. When you've reached your desired thickness, place the rolling pin in the middle and gently fold the crust over the rolling pin. Lift the dough onto your pie plate and unfold it.

5. Pre-baked crusts: Sometimes a recipe will call for a pre-baked crust. Some people place "weights" (either little balls specifically designed for this purpose, or even beans) in the pie crust to keep it from puffing and shrinking, but we've found that with this recipe, we don't need them. Just prick the bottom of the crust with a fork and bake at 450 degrees F. for 10–12 minutes or until golden brown.

6. Double crusts: Sometimes you'll need or want a second crust on top of a pie. Just double the recipe for the crust and cut the dough in half, using one part for the bottom and one part for the top.

When you put the crust on top, you'll need some way of letting the steam out. You can use miniature cookie cutters or a knife to cut cute shapes or decorations into the crust; some people cut some decorative slits so when you put it on top, it spreads a little and looks all pretty. Our favorite thing to do is a lattice top (see directions on page 223).

Apple Pie

Serves 8

☆ **Make Ahead**

●●●●●●●●●●●●●●●●

TIP: If your crust starts getting too brown, cut a circle out of a square of foil and place it on the pie so the foil covers the edge of the pie.

Making pie from scratch may seem intimidating if you've never made it before, but this is a great recipe to start with. The tender, flaky pie crust filled with fresh apples and classic spices will take you back to your grandma's kitchen.

Double Pastry Crust (p. 220)

6 cups peeled, sliced Granny Smith apples (about 1½ pounds)

1 tablespoon lemon juice

½ cup sugar

½ cup brown sugar

2 tablespoons all-purpose flour

½ teaspoon ground cinnamon

¼ teaspoon ground nutmeg

2 tablespoons butter, chopped

1. Roll half of the pastry to ⅛-inch thickness on a surface that's been sprayed with cooking spray. Gently place in a 9-inch pie plate; set aside.

2. Preheat your oven to 450 degrees F. Combine apples and lemon juice in a large bowl. Combine sugars, flour, and spices, mixing well. Spoon over apple mixture, tossing gently. Spoon filling evenly into pastry shell and dot with chopped butter.

3. Roll remaining pie crust ⅛-inch thick and cut a few slits or use decorative cookie cutters to make vent holes. Place over the pie and press the edges to seal. If you'd like to make a lattice crust, see the tutorial on page 223. You can brush the top of your crust with some melted butter and sprinkle with sugar.

4. Bake at 450 degrees F. for 15 minutes. Reduce heat to 350 degrees F. and bake 50 minutes more. If the crust starts getting too brown, see tip at left for how to make a shield.

5. Remove from oven and allow to cool for at least 15–20 minutes. Serve with vanilla ice cream or Sweetened Whipped Cream (p. 252).

How to Make a Lattice Crust

1. Place the rolled-out bottom crust in the pie plate, fill your pie as desired, and then roll out the top crust and cut it into strips about 1 inch wide. You can use a knife or a fluted pastry wheel.

2. Lay 4–5 strips vertically on top of your pie.

3. Fold every other strip back and lay a horizontal strip right under the part you've folded back.

4. Unfold the vertical strip so it lays on top of the horizontal strip. Repeat this step, this time folding back pieces that you didn't fold before and then continue repeating until the pie is covered.

5. Now gently press the crust strips into the bottom crust and finish the edges however you like! This step goes for any way you top your pie. We like to fold the strips into the edges to get a nice, round, solid edge and then flute the edges all the way around.

⊙ **Quick and Easy**

☆ **Make Ahead**

●●●●●●●●●●●●●●●

TIP: Chilling this pie is really important for the flavor and texture.

Banana Cream Pie

This is hands-down the best (and easiest!) banana cream pie we've ever had! Don't forget to check out all the variations like the Chunky Monkey variation we have pictured!

1 (3.4-ounce) box of instant chocolate or vanilla pudding mix

1 cup cold water

1 (14-ounce) can sweetened condensed milk

1 pint heavy whipping cream

2 (6-ounce) purchased cookie crusts. You can use anything—graham crackers, Nilla Wafers, shortbread, even Oreo.

2 large or 4 small bananas (approximately)

⅓ cup powdered sugar

1. In a medium bowl, combine pudding mix, cold water, and sweetened condensed milk. Mix well and place in the refrigerator to chill for a few minutes.

2. In another bowl, whip 1 cup of cream until soft peaks form. Fold into the pudding mixture and then return the mixture to the refrigerator.

3. Slice the bananas and layer them on the bottom of the crusts. Be sure to save the plastic domes that come with the pie crusts—you'll need them later! Set aside.

4. Now divide the pudding mixture between the two pie crusts.

5. In a medium bowl, whip the remaining whipping cream with ⅓ cup of powdered sugar until soft peaks form and then spread it on top of the two pies. Place the clear plastic shells back on the pies and refrigerate for several hours.

Chunky Monkey

Blend ½ cup creamy peanut butter into the pudding mixture before you fold in the whipped cream. Continue as directed, using a chocolate cookie crust. Sprinkle with honey-roasted peanuts just before serving.

Chocolate-Strawberry Trifle

Bake a 9 x 13-inch pan of brownies from a brownie mix or your favorite recipe. When cool, cut into cubes. Slice 1 pint of strawberries. Prepare the sweetened whipped cream and the banana cream pie filling made with chocolate pudding. In a trifle dish, make a layer of pudding, then brownie cubes, whipped cream, and then strawberries. Repeat as necessary (how many layers you have will depend on the size of your trifle dish).

Mississippi Mud Pie

Preheat oven to 375 degrees F. In a food processor, process 1 (16-ounce) package of Pecan Sandies cookies until crumbly. Mix with 1½ tablespoons of melted butter and then press lightly into a 9 x 13-inch dish. Bake in preheated oven for 10 minutes or until lightly browned. Remove from oven and allow to cool. Prepare the sweetened whipped cream and the pie filling with chocolate pudding. Spread the chocolate mixture over the pecan crust and then spread with the layer of whipped cream. Top with chocolate shavings or colored sprinkles.

How to Make a Pie in a Jar

We never, ever expected this to be hands-down our most popular post on the blog. These single serving pies can be prepped and then stored in the freezer until a craving strikes. They're also great baked up for neighbor gifts, teacher gifts, or I'd-like-to-be-out-of-the-doghouse gifts . . .

WIDE-MOUTH JARS. You want the short, squatty ones with sides that go straight up and down from top to bottom.

PIE CRUST DOUGH. You can either use the homemade pie crust dough on p. 220 or just buy a roll of pre-packaged dough. Either will make approximately 4 pies.

2 CUPS PREPARED FRUIT (pitted, diced, peeled, etc.).

2 TABLESPOONS SUGAR, brown or granulated (use more or less depending on sweetness of fruit).

2 TABLESPOONS FLOUR (again, more if your fruit is super juicy like cherries, less if it's pretty dry).

SEASONINGS AND FLAVORINGS (cinnamon, nutmeg, vanilla and almond extract, citrus zest, etc.).

1 TABLESPOON BUTTER (divided among the pies).

1. Roll out a ¼-inch thick piece of dough into an 8 x 8-inch square. Using the metal ring from the top of your jar as a cookie cutter, cut out 4 circles of dough.

2. Use the rest of the dough to line the jars. Break the dough into small pieces and press them along the inside of the jar, making sure the dough is pressed all the way up to the top of the jar.

3. Combine prepared fruit, sugar, flour, and seasoning. Fill the pies. Each pie will hold approximately ½ cup of pie filling. Use either filling below, or pick a favorite flavor of canned filling.

4. The dough circles you set aside will need vents so steam can escape. Use a knife to make a couple of slits or a tiny cookie cutter to make it decorative. When your topper is ready, slip it onto the top of the pie. Gently press down so the edges of the circle are completely inside the jar. Use your fingers, or a fork, to press the dough from the top into the dough on the edge of the jar to seal. If desired, brush the top with a little melted butter and a sprinkle of sugar.

Or, if you prefer, skip the dough topper and try the crumb topping, or top the pies with a mini lattice crust (see p. 223 for instructions).

5. Preheat oven to 375 degrees F. Place open jars on a baking sheet and bake for 45–55 minutes or until tops are golden brown.

FREEZER INSTRUCTIONS: Once pies are prepared through step 4, they can be frozen and kept for 2–3 months. To freeze, place metal tops on pies and screw the rings on securely. Place pies in freezer.

To cook from frozen, remove pie from freezer and place on baking sheet. Remove both the metal ring and the metal top. Place pie in oven and then turn heat to 375 degrees F. Bake for 50–60 minutes or until tops are golden brown.

Apple Pie Filling

2 cups diced, peeled tart green apples

1 tablespoon fresh lemon juice

2 tablespoons sugar

2 tablespoons flour

¼ teaspoon cinnamon

1 tablespoon butter, chopped into small pieces and divided among 4 pies

Toss all ingredients together and stir to combine. Divide mixture among the pies and dot the pies with butter.

Crumb Topping

Makes topping for 4–6 pies

¼ cup brown sugar

¼ cup flour

¾ teaspoon cinnamon

3 tablespoons cold butter

2 tablespoons oats

Combine sugar, flour, and cinnamon. Cut in the butter with two knives or a pastry blender. Add oats and stir to combine.

Makes 10 tarts or 1 9-inch pie

☆ **Make Ahead**
☺ **Quick and Easy**

●●●●●●●●●●●●●●●

TIP: You can also make this into a 9-inch pie by using a store-bought graham cracker crust and baking for 15 minutes.

Key Lime Tarts

One bite of this will transport you to the tropics. These little tarts are great for parties because people can mingle while they're eating their dessert.

5 egg yolks

1 (14-ounce) can sweetened condensed milk

About ½ cup fresh lime juice (key limes or regular limes)

10 mini graham cracker crusts (available near the regular graham cracker crusts in the baking aisle)

2 drops green food coloring, optional

1. Preheat oven to 350 degrees F.

2. In a medium bowl, combine the egg yolks, sweetened condensed milk, and lime juice. Distribute evenly among pie crusts (a cookie scoop works great for this).

3. Place tart pans on a large baking sheet and bake 10–11 minutes. Remove from oven and allow to cool; chill in refrigerator until ready to serve. Serve each tart with a dollop of Sweetened Whipped Cream (p. 252).

Mini Cheesecake Tarts

These perfectly portioned little cheesecakes are great finger food for big parties! Try finding holiday colors for celebrations—cherry and blueberry for the 4th of July or orange curd and dark chocolate for Halloween.

Makes 12 tarts

☆ **Make Ahead**

●●●●●●●●●●●●●●●●●

TIP: Foil liners are pretty and help these cheesecakes maintain their shape.

2 (8-ounce) packages cream cheese, softened

¾ cup sugar

2 tablespoons flour

¼ teaspoon baking powder

2 eggs

1 tablespoon fresh lemon juice

1½ teaspoons vanilla

Foil cupcake liners

12 Nilla Wafer Cookies

Optional toppings: canned pie filling, fresh berries, Sweetened Whipped Cream (p. 252), chocolate sauce, caramel sauce, lemon curd

1. Preheat oven to 375 degrees F.

2. With an electric mixer, beat cream cheese and sugar. Add in flour and baking powder and beat to combine. Then add in eggs, one at a time, lemon juice, and vanilla. Beat to combine.

3. Fill a muffin pan with foil cupcake liners and place one vanilla wafer in the bottom of each one. Divide batter between 12 muffin papers, filling each cup up to about ¼ inch from the top. Bake for 15–18 minutes or until a toothpick inserted into the middle comes out clean. They'll puff way up during baking, but they'll settle after being chilled.

4. Remove the pan from the oven and place it on a cooling rack. Let the cheesecakes cool completely. While they cool, they will sink down in the center. It's totally normal and it makes a perfect little well to fill up with the fruit filling. Before you add the filling, chill in the fridge for at least 4–6 hours or preferably overnight. Top as desired and serve.

TIP: To get crumbs for cookie crusts, you can either place the cookies in a food processor and process them until you have enough crumbs or place them in a heavy-duty zip-top bag and roll them with a rolling pin.

Pumpkin Cheesecake with Pecan-Gingersnap Crust

Forget pumpkin pie—this cool, creamy, slightly spiced pumpkin cheesecake will be the new favorite Thanksgiving dessert.

Crust

1¾ cups gingersnap crumbs (about 30 small cookies; see tip at left)

¾ cup ground pecans

6 tablespoons butter (no substitutions), melted

3 tablespoons brown sugar

Filling

6 ounces white chocolate (or 1 cup white chocolate chips)

3 (8-ounce) packages cream cheese

1 cup sugar

3 eggs

¾ cup canned pumpkin purée

2 teaspoons vanilla

¼ teaspoon nutmeg

1½ teaspoons cinnamon

⅛ teaspoon cloves

Topping

1 recipe Sweetened Whipped Cream (p. 252)

⅓ cup roughly chopped pecans, either toasted or candied (p. 254)

2 tablespoons bottled caramel sauce

1. Preheat oven to 350 degrees F. Using 2 large pieces of heavy-duty foil, securely wrap the bottom and outside of your cheesecake pan. This will prevent leaks when using the water bath. Alternately, you can tuck a turkey roasting bag around the pan to prevent water from leaking into the pan.

2. To make the crust, crush the gingersnaps (see the tip at left). Finely chop the pecans (in a food processor if you have one). Combine gingersnaps, pecans, brown sugar, and butter well. Evenly press the crumbs on the bottom and about 1 inch up the sides of a 9-inch springform pan.

3. To melt the white chocolate, place in a microwave-safe bowl and microwave in 30-second intervals, stirring in between, until smooth. Set aside.

   With an electric mixer beat cream cheese and sugar until smooth. Add eggs one at a time. Add pumpkin, vanilla, nutmeg, cinnamon, and cloves.

4. With the mixer running, slowly and steadily add in white chocolate in a steady stream. Pour the filling mixture on top of the crust.

5. Place the cheesecake pan inside a larger pan that's at least 2–3 inches deep. Place in the preheated oven. With a kettle or pitcher filled with hot water, pour water into the larger pan about halfway up the sides of the springform pan, or approximately 1½ to 2 inches.

6. Bake for 60–75 minutes or until set. The center should be slightly jiggly for the best texture.

7. When it's done, remove from oven and place on a rack until completely cool. Refrigerate for at least 12 hours. This is a very soft cheesecake so sufficient chilling is very important.

8. When ready to serve, spread sweetened whipped cream on top, drizzle caramel sauce over it, and sprinkle with pecans.

Strawberry-Lime Shortcakes with Coconut Cream

Use scones, angel food cake, or pound cake in this tropical twist on a classic treat!

6 slices of Sour Cream Pound Cake (p. 42)

4 cups sliced fresh strawberries

½ cup granulated sugar

4 tablespoons fresh-squeezed lime juice (about 2 limes)

¾ cup toasted coconut (see below)

Coconut Whipped Cream

1 cup heavy whipping cream

½ cup powdered sugar

2 teaspoons coconut extract

1 teaspoon vanilla

1. Mix sliced strawberries, sugar, and lime juice. Stir well and set aside. Stir occasionally over about 15 minutes. You want the sugar to dissolve and form a light syrup.

2. For the Coconut Whipped Cream, pour cream into a bowl and beat with an electric mixer for about one minute. Slowly add powdered sugar and both extracts. Continue beating until soft peaks form.

3. Slice cake and spoon a layer of strawberries and lime syrup on top. Top with a generous dollop of Coconut Whipped Cream and sprinkle with toasted coconut.

Toasted Coconut

1. Preheat oven to 375 degrees F.

2. Spread desired amount of sweetened coconut onto a cookie sheet or other oven-safe dish. If your coconut is unsweetened, you can toss it with a little powdered sugar first.

3. Place in the oven and cook for about 2–5 minutes depending on how much you're doing. It's important to stir often, about every 30 seconds, especially when it starts to brown. The coconut will be dry and lightly browned.

☆ **Make Ahead**
⏲ **Quick and Easy**

●●●●●●●●●●●●●●●●

TIP: To measure out 2 tablespoons of boiling water, heat a larger amount of water in a microwave safe dish to boiling and then measure out 2 tablespoons and discard the rest.

Easy Chocolate Mousse

This light and fluffy chocolate mousse is stabilized with gelatin and can also be used to fill Cream Puffs (p. 239) or as the mousse layer in the Chocolate Mousse Crunch Cake (p. 236). Try it with a dollop of whipped cream and some fresh berries for an easy, yet elegant dessert.

1 teaspoon unflavored gelatin

1 tablespoon cold water

2 tablespoons boiling water (just heat it in a small bowl in your microwave)

½ cup sugar

¼ cup unsweetened cocoa powder

1 cup heavy whipping cream

1 teaspoon vanilla

1. In a small bowl, combine gelatin and cold water and allow to stand for about 1 minute. While gelatin is softening, bring 2 tablespoons water to a boil in the microwave (see tip at left). Whisk into the softened gelatin and allow to cool.

2. In a medium mixing bowl, combine sugar, cocoa powder, cream, and vanilla. Beat with an electric mixer until medium-stiff peaks form. Mix in gelatin mixture until combined and refrigerate for 30 minutes. If serving in individual cups, place mousse in cups or bowls before refrigerating.

Carrot Cake

Moist and rich, this classic cake is topped with a to-die-for cream cheese icing. And because this is a sheet cake rather than a layer cake, it's easy to transport to parties and potlucks.

Serves 12

☆ **Make Ahead**
⏱ **Quick and Easy**

ROLLOVER
Buttermilk

●●●●●●●●●●●●●●●●

TIP: The eggs need to be at room temperature for this cake, so to quickly warm them up, place them in a bowl of warm (but not hot) water for 10–15 minutes.

2¼ cups flour

2 teaspoons baking soda

1½ teaspoons cinnamon

½ teaspoon nutmeg

½ teaspoon salt

1 cup butter-flavored shortening

1½ cups sugar

3 eggs, room temperature

¾ cup buttermilk

2 cups shredded carrots

1½ cups coconut

¾ cup chopped walnuts

½ cup raisins, optional

Cream Cheese Frosting

2 (8-ounce) packages of cream cheese

½ cup butter, softened

16 ounces powdered sugar

2 teaspoons vanilla

1 teaspoon almond extract, optional

1. Preheat oven to 325 degrees F.

2. Combine flour, baking soda, cinnamon, nutmeg, and salt in a bowl.

3. Beat shortening and sugar until fluffy. Add room-temperature eggs one at a time, beating after each addition.

4. Alternately add the flour mixture and the buttermilk, starting and ending with flour. Gently stir in carrots, coconut, walnuts, and raisins (if desired).

5. Pour the batter into a 9 x 13-inch pan sprayed with cooking spray and bake for 55–65 minutes. Cool and frost with cream cheese frosting. Top with additional chopped walnuts if desired.

6. For the Cream Cheese Frosting, beat cream cheese and butter at medium speed with an electric mixer until creamy. Gradually add powdered sugar, beating until fluffy. Stir in vanilla and almond extracts. This makes a lot of frosting—use it all if you love the frosting or spread it on cookies, cupcakes, or between graham crackers.

●●●●●●●●●●●●●●●●●

TIP: If you don't use all the mousse, you can make individual parfaits with the leftover mousse, Heath bits, and the cake left over after leveling the layers.

Chocolate Mousse Crunch Cake

This special-occasion cake will wow your guests both visually and by how amazing it tastes! For an extra special birthday, try to find some long sparkler candles.

1 package Duncan Hines Devil's Food Cake

Crushed Heath bars or a bag of Heath bits

1 recipe Easy Chocolate Mousse (p. 234)

Ganache

½ cup dark or semisweet chocolate chips

½ cup heavy cream

1. Bake cake according to cake mix instructions in 2 8-inch round pans. Allow to cool and set aside. This can be done several days in advance; just freeze the cakes when you're done.

2. To prepare the ganache, combine the chocolate chips and cream in a microwave-safe bowl. Heat on high for 3–4 minutes, stirring the mixture after each minute and being sure to scrape the bottom of the bowl, until the mixture is completely smooth. If it is too thin, the ganache can be refrigerated until the desired consistency is reached.

3. With a serrated knife, carefully slice the roundest part of each cake layer off so the layers are level. Place one layer on the serving plate and spread about ½ (or all) of the chocolate mousse over the cake. Sprinkle with Heath bits. Place second layer on top of Heath bits.

4. Spoon the ganache over the top layer, allowing it to drip down the sides. Sprinkle with additional Heath bits and refrigerate until ready to serve.

☆ **Make Ahead**
☉ **Quick and Easy**

ROLLOVER
Buttermilk

●●●●●●●●●●●●●●●●

TIP: This cake can either be served warm and gooey (like in the picture) or you can make it a few hours ahead of time and allow the cake to cool completely and the frosting to set up.

Texas Sheet Cake

It wouldn't be a summer barbecue at Kate's house without this cake topped with a scoop of vanilla bean ice cream. She added the nuts to the recipe to appease her dad, but she likes it better without them.

½ cup real butter
½ cup butter-flavored shortening
2 (1-ounce) squares baking chocolate
1 cup water
2 cups flour
1 teaspoon baking soda
2 cups sugar
½ cup buttermilk
2 eggs, beaten
1 teaspoon cinnamon
1 teaspoon vanilla

Frosting
6 tablespoons milk
2 (1-ounce) squares baking chocolate
½ cup butter
1 pound powdered sugar
1 teaspoon vanilla
½ cup chopped pecans or walnuts, optional

1. Preheat oven to 350 degrees F. Grease an 11 x 17-inch jelly roll pan (or you can use a 9 x 13-inch pan, but you may die of sugar shock—there's something to be said for spreading the love in this recipe).

2. Combine butter, shortening, chocolate, and water in a small saucepan. Heat until chocolate is melted.

3. In a separate small bowl, combine flour and baking soda. Set aside.

4. In a large mixing bowl, combine sugar, buttermilk, eggs, cinnamon, and vanilla. Combine with chocolate mixture. Add flour mixture and mix very well. Pour into pan and bake 20–25 minutes or until a pick comes out clean. Five minutes before cake is done, make frosting.

5. For the frosting, combine milk, chocolate, and butter in a medium-large saucepan. Heat until bubbles form around the edge.

6. Remove from heat and add powdered sugar and vanilla and beat until smooth. If desired, add 1 cup chopped pecans or walnuts. While icing is still warm, pour over cake.

Cream Puffs

Don't be scared about making homemade cream puffs—these are incredibly easy and everyone will be impressed by your ability to make pastry! You could fill these with anything—pudding, strawberry cream, Bavarian cream, or even whipped flavored cream cheese.

½ cup water

¼ cup butter

⅛ teaspoon salt

½ cup flour

2 eggs

1 recipe Easy Chocolate Mousse (p. 234)

1. Preheat oven to 400 degrees F.

2. In a medium saucepan, combine water, butter, and salt and bring to a boil. Remove from heat and add flour all at once. Stir quickly with a spoon until dough forms a ball.

3. Add one egg at a time, combining completely after each addition. The mixture will be very smooth and velvety.

4. Either drop the dough by scant teaspoons or spoon dough into a pastry bag and pipe it directly onto an ungreased baking sheet. Teaspoons seem small, but the pastry will puff up and still be bite-sized.

5. Bake for 20–25 minutes or until golden brown. Remove from oven, allow to cool for a few minutes, and then transfer to a wire rack to cool completely.

6. While the pastry is baking, prepare the chocolate mousse.

7. When the mousse has chilled and the puffs have cooled, fill a decorating bag fitted with a large tip with the mousse.

8. Gently insert the piping tip into the bottom of each pastry puff and squeeze filling into puff, being careful not to overfill. Sprinkle with powdered sugar or dip the top in chocolate and refrigerate until ready to serve. Makes about 40 bite-sized cream puffs.

Makes about 40 bite-sized cream puffs

☆ **Make Ahead**

●●●●●●●●●●●●●●

TIP: These are actually better the next day, so if you're throwing a party, making them ahead of time should ease your workload. Store them in an airtight container.

Generously frosts 12 cupcakes or a 9 x 13-inch sheet cake

●●●●●●●●●●●●●●●●

TIP: Use real, high-quality, name brand butter. Cover leftovers and store at room temperature.

Whipped Buttercream Frosting

Hands-down our favorite frosting. Ever. It has some surprise ingredients that make it light, fluffy, not too sweet, and velvety smooth. It's sure to win over nonlovers of frosting everywhere!

3 tablespoons flour

½ cup milk

½ cup real butter

½ cup granulated sugar

1 teaspoon vanilla extract (almond, lemon, orange, or pretty much any other flavor is also delicious)

1. Whisk together the flour and the milk in a small saucepan and cook, whisking constantly, over medium heat until it starts to thicken. It should look like pudding—you should be able to see the bottom of the pan when you stir it.

2. Press the mixture through a mesh strainer and then let it cool completely to room temperature or chill it in the fridge. It needs to be cooled completely or it will melt the butter and you'll have runny frosting.

3. In an electric stand mixer, beat the butter and the sugar for a minute or two with the whisk attachment until the mixture is well-combined and fluffy.

4. While the mixer is running, add in the thickened milk mixture and the flavoring. Beat for 7 minutes on the highest speed you can without spraying it all over the place. It may look curdled at first, and it may take up to 12 minutes. If you have to beat the frosting longer than 7 minutes, try placing an ice pack on the bowl to keep it cool.

5. When the frosting is velvety smooth and perfectly fluffy, use it to fill cupcakes or other pastries or as a frosting on top.

Frozen Pudding Pops

These aren't your typical pudding pops! We've included some of our favorite flavor combinations, but feel free to use these as inspiration to invent your own!

Mint-Chocolate Cookie Pudding Pops

1 (1-ounce) box sugar-free instant chocolate pudding mix

¼ teaspoon peppermint extract

1¾ cups half-and-half

10 Oreo cookies, crushed (about 1 heaping cup)

Blend pudding mix, extract, and half-and-half in a blender until smooth. Stir in crushed cookies by hand. Spoon into molds and freeze.

Blueberry-Lemon Cheesecake Pudding Pops

1 (1-ounce) box sugar-free cheesecake instant pudding mix

1¾ cups half-and-half

1 teaspoon lemon zest

1 cup blueberries

In a blender, mix cheesecake pudding mix and half-and-half until smooth. Add in lemon zest and blueberries and pulse a couple of times to break up the blueberries. Spoon into molds and freeze.

Cherry Almond Fudge Pudding Pops

1 (1-ounce) box sugar-free instant chocolate fudge pudding mix

1¾ cups half-and-half

¼ teaspoon almond extract

About 20 cherries (1¼ cups) pitted and halved

⅓ cup miniature chocolate chips

Blend pudding mix, half-and-half, and almond extract in blender until smooth. Add in cherries and pulse 2–3 times. Stir in chocolate chips by hand. Spoon into in molds and freeze.

Piña Colada Pudding Pops

1 (1-ounce) box sugar-free instant coconut pudding mix

1 (13.5-ounce) can coconut milk

1 tablespoon fresh lime juice

1 (8-ounce) can crushed pineapple, drained

⅓ cup shredded coconut

Coconut extract, optional (the coconut flavor is pretty mild, so if you want a little kick, add some coconut extract)

Blend pudding mix, coconut milk, and lime juice in a blender until smooth. Add crushed pineapple and shredded coconut and pulse a couple of times to incorporate. Add extract if desired. Spoon into in molds and freeze.

Peanut Butter Banana Pudding Pops

1 (1-ounce) box sugar-free instant vanilla pudding mix

1¾ cups milk

1 ripe banana (see tip at right)

¼ cup peanut butter

Blend all ingredients until smooth. Spoon into in molds and freeze.

Strawberries and Cream Pudding Pops

12 medium strawberries (about 1¾–2 cups of roughly chopped berries)

2–3 tablespoons sugar

1 (1-ounce) box sugar-free instant vanilla pudding mix

6 ounces vanilla yogurt (strawberry is great too)

1 cup milk

Remove stems from berries and pulse with 2 tablespoons sugar in a food processor until completely smooth. Taste and add more sugar if needed. You should have just over a cup of purée. Set aside.

In a blender combine pudding mix, yogurt, and milk and blend until combined. Layer or swirl the pudding mixture with the strawberry mixture in popsicle molds and freeze until solid.

TIP: Bananas that aren't quite ripe taste especially bitter when frozen, so make sure you use a sweet, ripe banana.

Serves 2–3

⊙ **Quick and Easy**

●●●●●●●●●●●●●●●●●

TIP: For all but the most powerful blenders, you'll generally get better results by blending all the ingredients except the ice cream and then mashing softened ice cream in by hand after everything else has been mixed.

Pumpkin Pie Milkshake

Even if you're not crazy about pumpkin pie (like Sara), this festive, spiced milkshake is guaranteed to be a hit. It's one of Sara's favorite family night treats during the fall and winter months!

⅓ cup pumpkin purée

¼–½ cup milk

¼ teaspoon vanilla

½ teaspoon cinnamon

Pinch of cloves

Pinch of nutmeg

2 tablespoons brown sugar

2 cups vanilla ice cream

1–2 graham crackers, crushed

1. Combine all the ingredients, except the graham crackers, in the blender and blend until the desired consistency is reached. Add more milk if desired.

2. Pour into individual serving glasses, sprinkle with graham cracker crumbs, and serve immediately.

Mango-Pineapple Sorbet

Using canned crushed pineapple brings this sorbet together in a matter of a few tasty minutes.

3 cups diced mango (about 3 medium mangoes)

¾ cup sugar

¼ cup fresh lime juice

1 (8-ounce) can crushed pineapple, including juice

1. In a food processor (or good blender), purée the mangoes. Add the sugar and lime juice and process to combine. Transfer to a large bowl and stir in the pineapple with the juice.

2. Pour the mixture into an ice cream maker (see tip at right if you don't have an ice cream maker) and freeze according to the manufacturer's instructions for about 30 minutes or until the sorbet is frozen (but still soft). Transfer to an airtight container and freeze until ready to serve.

3. To serve the following day, set out on counter for about 15 minutes to soften.

Makes about 3 cups

☆ **Make Ahead**

●●●●●●●●●●●●●●●●●

TIP: If you don't have an ice cream maker, just place sorbet in an airtight container and put it in the freezer. Take it out and stir once an hour for 3 hours, or until it's too hard to stir.

☆ **Make Ahead**

TIP: Test the custard mixture by dipping a spoon in and then running your finger down the back of the spoon. When your finger leaves a track, it's ready.

How to Pit a Cherry

1. Remove the stem from the cherry.

2. If you're right-handed, grab a cherry with your left hand. In your right hand, hold a bamboo skewer, chopstick, or straw. Holding both firmly, poke the stick/skewer through the indentation where the stem was until it hits the pit. Then just give it a push and it will pop right out the other side.

Cherry Chocolate Ice Cream

Sweet, fresh cherries combine with a frozen custard and dark chocolate in this treat that's a taste of summer. For extra chocolate, drizzle with Hot Fudge Sauce (p. 252).

1½ cups 2% milk

1 cup sugar

2 eggs

1 cup heavy cream

2 cups cherries, pitted and halved or quartered (see tutorial at left)

½ teaspoon pure vanilla extract

½ teaspoon pure almond extract

1 (4.5-ounce) dark chocolate bar (about 1 cup shavings; you can grate them in your food processor)

1. Combine the milk and sugar in a medium saucepan. Heat over medium until bubbles form around the edges. Remove from heat.

2. In a small mixing bowl, whisk the eggs thoroughly. Very slowly, add ½ of the hot milk mixture, whisking the eggs constantly. Return the pan with remaining milk mixture to stove top and then whisk the egg and milk mixture back into the saucepan, whisking constantly. Be careful not to heat the eggs too hot too fast, or they'll curdle.

3. Add the heavy cream. Over medium-low heat and stirring constantly, continue heating the custard mixture to 160 degrees F. It will start to thicken quickly (see tip at left).

4. Once ready, remove from heat and add the chopped cherries immediately. Add vanilla and almond extracts as well. Let the custard cool (you can use an ice bath if you want to speed that process up) and then refrigerate, covered, for several hours.

5. Once the custard is chilled, transfer the mixture to an ice cream maker and churn according to manufacturer's instructions.

6. While the ice cream is churning, grate the chocolate. Add the chocolate shavings into the ice cream when there's just a few minutes left. If you wait too long and it's already too thick to really mix it well, just stir them in by hand as you transfer your ice cream into another container. Freeze for several hours before serving. Makes 1½ quarts.

☆ **Make Ahead**

●●●●●●●●●●●●●●●●

TIP: The roasted bananas in this recipe make the ice cream incredibly soft and smooth, but the ice cream may be softer than usual when coming straight out of your ice cream maker. Plan enough time to let the ice cream set in the freezer for several hours before eating.

Caramelized Banana Ice Cream

This is a great way to use up bananas that are about to become over-ripe. Serve with a drizzle of Buttermilk Caramel Syrup (p. 70).

4 very ripe bananas, sliced into ½–1-inch segments

¼ cup brown sugar

1 teaspoon cinnamon

1 tablespoon real butter, melted

2 cups heavy cream

1 cup whole milk

½ cup granulated sugar

¼ teaspoon salt

2 teaspoons vanilla

1. Preheat oven to 400 degrees F.

2. Line a 9 x 13-inch baking dish with foil and place bananas in it. Sprinkle brown sugar, cinnamon, and melted butter over bananas and toss well with hands. Spread bananas out in a single layer.

3. Bake bananas for 15 minutes. Stir, and bake for 15 minutes more. Remove from oven and allow to cool.

4. While the bananas are cooking, combine cream, whole milk, granulated sugar, salt, and vanilla. Whisk until sugar is dissolved. Refrigerate until completely chilled.

5. When the bananas are completely cooled, purée them with all of the syrup from the pan in a food processor or blender until completely smooth. Whisk purée into the milk mixture until combined. Chill entire mixture.

6. Churn in an ice cream maker according to the manufacturer's instructions and transfer to an airtight, freezer-safe container. Freeze for several hours to set.

Rocky Road Ice Cream

This classic ice cream is enhanced with brown sugar and toasted pecans. Scoop it into old-fashioned waffle cones during a summer party like a 4th of July barbecue.

Makes 1 quart

☆ **Make Ahead**

ROLLOVER
Pecans

2 cups heavy cream

¾ cup low-fat milk

¼ cup granulated sugar

⅓ cup brown sugar

½ tablespoon vanilla

¼ cup unsweetened cocoa powder

½ cup chopped pecans, toasted

1 cup mini marshmallows

1. Gently whisk cream, milk, sugars, vanilla, and cocoa powder by hand for about 2 minutes to incorporate the cocoa powder and dissolve the sugars.

2. Freeze in an ice cream maker according to the manufacturer's instructions.

3. When the ice cream has finished churning, fold in the pecans and marshmallows by hand and transfer to a freezer container. Freeze for 1–2 hours or until desired consistency is reached.

Makes 1½ quarts

☆ **Make Ahead**

TIP: Don't toss those scraps when you make Sugar Cookies (p. 208)—bake them up and use them as the cookies in this recipe!

Snickerdoodle Ice Cream

Chunks of sugar or shortbread cookies are frozen into cinnamon custard ice cream for a light-tasting treat that can be served all year long.

1½ cups 2% milk

1 cup sugar

2 eggs, room temperature

1 cup heavy cream

2 teaspoons cinnamon

1 teaspoon vanilla

About 1½–2 cups chopped Sugar Cookies (p. 208), snickerdoodles, or shortbread cookies

1. Combine milk and sugar in a medium saucepan. Heat over medium until bubbles form around the edges. Remove from heat.

2. In a small mixing bowl, whisk the eggs thoroughly. Very slowly, add ½ of the hot milk mixture, whisking the eggs constantly.

3. Return the pan with remaining milk mixture to stove top and then whisk the egg and milk mixture back into the saucepan, whisking constantly. Add the whipping cream. Over medium-low heat and stirring constantly, continue heating the custard mixture to 160 degrees F. It will start to thicken quickly; remove from heat when your finger leaves a track on a spoon coated in the custard mixture (see the tip in the Cherry Chocolate Ice Cream recipe, p. 246, for how to test a custard with your finger).

4. Whisk in cinnamon and vanilla. Place the custard in an airtight container and chill in the refrigerator several hours.

5. When ready to make the ice cream, pour the chilled custard into an ice cream maker and freeze according to the manufacturer's instructions. When the ice cream is almost done (the ice cream maker might be straining and the ice cream will look like soft serve), add chopped cookies. Transfer the ice cream to an airtight container and freeze at least 1–2 hours (but no longer than 4–5 days) before serving.

⊕ **Quick and Easy**

●●●●●●●●●●●●●●●●

TIP: To make an individual hot fudge serving, use the 3.5-ounce cans of sweetened condensed milk found in the Latin food aisle of the grocery store. In a microwave-safe dish, combine the condensed milk, 2 tablespoons chocolate chips, and 1 tablespoon butter and heat in the microwave in 30-second increments, stirring regularly until smooth.

SERVING SUGGESTIONS: Serve hot fudge sauce with ice cream or Cookie Sundae Cups (p. 213) or as a fondue. For hot fudge milk shakes, blend with vanilla ice cream and serve with an additional drizzle of hot fudge sauce, some Sweetened Whipped Cream, and a maraschino cherry.

Hot Fudge Sauce

Don't be fooled by how quick and easy this hot fudge sauce is—it's pretty much the best hot fudge sauce you'll ever try!

3 ounces semisweet or dark chocolate (3 [1-ounce] squares or ½ cup chips)

¼ cup butter

1 can sweetened condensed milk

1. If you're using squares of chocolate, chop into smaller pieces. Set aside.

2. In a small saucepan, heat the butter and condensed milk over medium-low until the butter melts and the milk is warm. Add the chocolate and stir until the chocolate is completely melted and smooth. Remove from heat.

3. Serve as desired. Store leftovers in an airtight container for 1–2 weeks.

Sweetened Whipped Cream

1 cup heavy whipping cream

⅓ cup powdered sugar

½ teaspoon vanilla, optional

Combine whipping cream and powdered sugar in a large bowl. With an electric hand mixer, beat until soft peaks form. Serve immediately.

Caramels

This is one classic candy that will never go out of style. This recipe is so easy and forgiving—it's a great candy for those who might feel nervous about whipping out that candy thermometer.

1 cup butter

2 cups sugar

2 cups light corn syrup

2 cups heavy whipping cream, divided

2 teaspoons vanilla

1. Combine butter, sugar, corn syrup, and 1 cup whipping cream in a large, heavy stockpot. Cook over medium-low heat, stirring gently, until sugar dissolves.

2. Turn heat to medium and cook until candy thermometer reaches 224 degrees F., stirring occasionally. Stir in the remaining 1 cup whipping cream. Continue to cook over medium heat until thermometer registers 245 degrees F. (soft ball stage). Add vanilla.

3. Pour mixture into a greased 9 x 13-inch pan. Cool overnight and then cut into squares. Wrap individually in wax paper.

Makes about 117 1 x 1-inch caramels

☆ **Make Ahead**

●●●●●●●●●●●●●●●

TIP: Wrapping a whole batch of caramels by yourself is a great way to go crazy. Enlist any little (or big) helpers you have lying around the house! Also, for easy removal from the pan (and cleanup), try laying two pieces of parchment or wax paper crosswise in the 9 x 13-inch pan, leaving about 1 inch of overhang. When the caramels have cooled, you can lift the sheet of candy straight out of the pan.

VARIATION: After the caramels have cooled and been cut, try dipping some halfway or completely in melted chocolate. Place the dipped caramels on a sheet of wax paper sprayed with nonstick cooking spray. If desired, sprinkle with kosher or coarse sea salt for a gourmet treat.

Candied Nuts

These sweet nuts add flavor and texture to salads like the Steak and Mango Salad on p. 138, but they're also a great crunchy snack by themselves or even packaged up for holiday gifts!

¼ cup brown sugar

1 tablespoon light corn syrup

1 tablespoon butter

1 cup nuts

¼ teaspoon cinnamon, optional

1. In a nonstick skillet, heat the brown sugar, corn syrup, and butter over medium heat, stirring as the mixture comes together and bubbles. Add the nuts and stir to coat.

2. Continue cooking for 5–7 minutes, stirring constantly until nuts turn golden brown and smell toasted.

3. Transfer to foil, waxed paper, or parchment and cool completely.

4. Break them apart with your fingers and enjoy!

Easy Pretzel Turtles

You'll make these easy, fun, addictive little treats over and over—for holidays, parties, or just hanging out with family or friends.

Makes about 55 candies

☆ **Make Ahead**
☉ **Quick and Easy**

About 55 small pretzels (as many as you have Rolos)

1 bag of Rolo candies (each bag has about 55 candies)

Pecan halves, salted peanuts, cashews, macadamia nuts, M&M's (all varieties), or miniature marshmallows

Almond bark or white chocolate for drizzling, optional

1. Preheat oven to 350 degrees F. Place the pretzels on a parchment-lined baking sheet. I like to use parchment paper for easy handling, but you can also put them on foil, a silicone mat, or directly onto the cookie sheet.

2. Unwrap your Rolo candies and place one on top of each pretzel.

3. Place the pan in the preheated oven for 3–4 minutes. You just want the chocolate on the outside to look glossy and like it's beginning to melt, but the candies should still hold their shape.

4. Remove pan from oven and gently press your desired toppings right into the center of the chocolate candy. This is where you can be creative—just top these off with anything that would work with the sweet, salty, chocolatey combination.

5. For extra-fancy presentation, melt some almond bark in a zip-top plastic bag and nip the corner off to drizzle. A little goes a long way—about ½ of a square will be more than enough to drizzle over the pretzels.

6. After snacking on a few with no one noticing, allow the rest to cool. Set out for snacking or place in treat boxes or bags for neighbor and teacher gifts.

Stovetop Kettle Corn

If you love fresh kettle corn but don't like the microwave variety and don't want to buy a kettle corn popper, this recipe, made with a regular heavy-duty pan, is the perfect solution!

3 tablespoons canola oil	3 tablespoons granulated sugar
⅓ cup popcorn kernels	Kosher salt

1. Place a large stockpot on the stove top. Set heat to medium-high. Add oil. While your oil is heating (it won't take long), measure out your popcorn into a small bowl. Add the sugar to the kernels. When it's time to cook, everything moves very quickly, so it's important to have it all ready to go.

2. Wait until you see your oil smoke. This is one little trick that a lot of people overlook, but it's important. The smoke is very faint, but if you just stare at the pot (it helps to get down parallel to it), you'll see little billows of smoke coming up. That's your cue!

3. Pour popcorn kernels and sugar into the pot.

4. Immediately stir using a wooden spoon or rubber spatula, scraping sugar from bottom of pan. This step should only take no more than 10 seconds—any longer than that and the kernels may start popping around.

5. Cover the pot with a tight-fitting lid. You will need to shake the pot with your hands and you'll want to make sure the lid stays on, so drape a kitchen towel over the lid and both handles. Hold the pot by the handles in a way that you're securing the lid on as well. Shake the pan side to side in all directions and up and down a few times. Do this every 20 seconds or so. It will keep the sugar from burning on the bottom and help the kernels to be evenly coated.

6. After a few minutes you should start hearing the pops. If it doesn't start popping after a few minutes, crack the lid to let some of the pressure out. Chances are when you put the lid back on, it will begin popping. Continue the shaking every 20 seconds or so until you can tell almost everything is popped. Remove the lid and stir immediately.

7. Sprinkle kosher salt to taste and then keep stirring. Toss in a serving bowl and serve immediately.

Cinnamon Bun Caramel Corn

This is one of our most beloved recipes. Try portioning this popcorn into individual cellophane bags and tying with cute ribbon for holiday gifts or for guests to grab and snack on at a party. Don't be surprised when you're hunted down for the recipe!

Makes 13 cups of popcorn or about 24 small, individual servings

☆ **Make Ahead**

●●●●●●●●●●●●●●●

TIP: You can use air-popped or microwave popcorn. If using microwave, try to find a natural flavor that's low in butter and salt.

12 cups popped popcorn (about ½ cup un-popped kernels, popped), see tip at right

1 cup roughly chopped pecans

1 cup brown sugar

¾ teaspoon cinnamon

½ cup real butter

¼ cup light corn syrup (honey makes a good substitution)

1 teaspoon vanilla

½ teaspoon baking soda

3 squares almond bark

1. Preheat oven to 250 degrees F.

2. Place popcorn and chopped pecans in a large bowl and set aside.

3. Combine the brown sugar and cinnamon in a 2-quart capacity microwave safe bowl. Mix well. Chop the butter into chunks and place on top of the sugar mixture. Pour corn syrup over everything. Microwave on high for 30 seconds and then stir to combine. Return to microwave and heat for 2 minutes. Remove and stir and then microwave for 2 minutes more.

4. Remove from microwave and add vanilla and baking soda. Stir to combine. The mixture will foam and rise. Pour the caramel mixture over the popcorn and pecans and stir very well so everything is well coated.

5. Spread popcorn mixture onto a foil-lined jelly roll pan. Place the pan in the oven and bake for 30 minutes, stirring every 10 minutes.

6. Remove the pan from the oven and spread mixture out on a large piece of parchment, waxed paper, or foil sprayed with nonstick cooking spray.

7. Melt the almond bark according to package instructions. Drizzle over popcorn mixture. When the almond bark is hardened and popcorn is cool, break into chunks and enjoy!

Rollover Ingredients

We've created this index to help you plan meals and use up perishable or uncommon ingredients.

Index

About the Authors

Sara Smith Wells was born and raised in the Seattle area. Inspired by the lush green surroundings of the Pacific Northwest, she earned a degree in horticulture from Brigham Young University and put her talents to work as a landscape designer. Her knack for design, as well as a lifetime passion for culinary exploration and entertaining on the spur-of-the-moment, resulted in catering opportunities, which allowed Sara to showcase her belief that food can taste great and be beautiful as well. She has since become an avid photographer and enjoyed styling and photographing the recipes in this book.

Sara served an LDS mission in Curitiba, Brazil, where she picked up a love of fresh ingredients and a taste for Latin flavor that influences much of her cooking today. She and her husband, Eric, currently reside in Boise, Idaho, where they cook, eat, laugh, and play with their three young sons, Tyler, Owen, and Jack.

Kate Randle Jones was born and raised in Logan, Utah, where she dabbled in cooking, but never seriously. After her sophomore year at Brigham Young University, she married Sam Jones, and they suddenly found themselves to be the stereotypical broke college student couple. Due to the fact that they needed to eat and she needed a hobby, Kate began cooking and baking nearly everything from scratch. Once she got comfortable in the kitchen, she started experimenting with different tastes, recipes, and methods.

She graduated from BYU in 2004 with a degree in English and considers herself beyond lucky that she gets to do her two favorite things: write and cook. In her spare time, she loves to read, entertain, and travel (or, at the very least, think about traveling!). She currently lives in an old house with a big yard in Louisiana with her husband, Sam; her son, Clark; and her daughter, Meredith.